# Praise for U~~~~~~

The anger that mothers feel is so c~~~~~~
Amber has written a sensitive and pow~~~~~~
hearts and give a gracious way to move to a relationship defined by gentleness and love. A wonderful book.

> **SALLY CLARKSON**, speaker, mentor, and bestselling author of over
> twenty books

How thankful I am for God's transforming Word and teachers like Amber
Lia who are willing to open up the Bible and apply it to the specific challenges
we face each day. For moms who struggle to parent with gentleness, with the
help of the Holy Spirit, and the guidance of God's holy Word, *UnTriggered*
is the daily devotional for you. Keep it bedside, along with your Bible. Seek
God first and often! Ask Him to illuminate your path as you parent, and He
will guide you as you go! There is hope for us. Change won't happen naturally, but it can happen supernaturally—and *UnTriggered* will help!

> **WENDY SPEAKE**, coauthor of *Triggers: Exchanging Parents' Angry*
> *Reactions for Gentle Biblical Responses* and host of *The 40 Day Sugar*
> *Fast*, wendyspeake.com

*UnTriggered* offers a lifeline of grace, not just for the mom who struggles
with anger, but also for the mom who feels overwhelmed, anxious, or
shamed by past actions. Amber Lia's gentle reminders to trust and rest in
the transformative power of God in our daily parenting journey offer a
comforting embrace to weary moms, inviting them to lean into the Father's
love even as they care for their families. With a mix of empowering stories,
practical prayers, and actionable next steps, this book will help moms re-
discover the delight of parenting and the goodness of God.

> **KRISTIN DEMERY**, author of *Merry & Bright: Rediscover the Hope,*
> *Peace, and Joy of Advent*

*UnTriggered* is a heartfelt companion for mothers at any stage of their journey. Each entry is filled with biblical encouragement and practical tips that resonate deeply with the challenges and joys of motherhood. The blend of faith and relatable advice makes it a source of comfort and wisdom. As a mom who has walked through those early years, I couldn't help but wish I had a resource like this back then. The devotionals are short yet impactful—perfect for a busy mom's schedule—and provide just the right balance of spiritual nourishment and practical guidance. If you're a mom looking for encouragement or a gift for a mother in your life, this devotional is a must-have. It will inspire you to embrace the highs and lows of motherhood with grace and faith.

**MACKI SMITH**, writer, girl-mom, and *The Peace-Seeking Woman* *amber* lia

A DEVOTIONAL

# *un*triggered

## 60 DAYS OF TRANSFORMATION
## FOR MOMS WHO STRUGGLE WITH ANGER

**MOODY PUBLISHERS**
CHICAGO

Unless otherwise indicated, all Scripture quotations are taken from the *Holy Bible*, New Living Translation, copyright © 1996, 2004, 2015 by Tyndale House Foundation. Used by permission of Tyndale House Publishers, Carol Stream, Illinois 60188. All rights reserved.

Scripture quotations marked (NIV) are taken from the Holy Bible, New International Version®, NIV®. Copyright © 1973, 1978, 1984, 2011 by Biblica, Inc.™ Used by permission of Zondervan. All rights reserved worldwide. www.zondervan.com The "NIV" and "New International Version" are trademarks registered in the United States Patent and Trademark Office by Biblica, Inc.™

Published in association with Books & Such Literary Management, www.booksandsuch.com.

Edited by Pamela Joy Pugh
Interior design: Puckett Smartt
Cover illustration and design: Good Mood Design Co / Riley Moody

Library of Congress Cataloging-in-Publication Data

Names: Lia, Amber, author.
Title: Untriggered : 60 days of transformation for moms who struggle with anger / Amber Lia.
Description: Chicago : Moody Publishers, [2025] | Summary: "This devotional touches on heart issues like releasing comparison with other moms, becoming a results-free mom, resisting comparison of children, embracing the gift of motherhood, and more. Your heavenly Father parents you with tenderness and patience. We can grow to be like Him. You can experience transformation and become untriggered"-- Provided by publisher.
Identifiers: LCCN 2024056607 (print) | LCCN 2024056608 (ebook) | ISBN 9780802433794 (paperback) | ISBN 9780802470980 (ebook)
Subjects: LCSH: Motherhood--Religious aspects--Christianity. | Anger--Psychological aspects.
Classification: LCC BV4529.18 .L53 2025 (print) | LCC BV4529.18 (ebook) | DDC 248.8/431--dc23/eng/20241227
LC record available at https://lccn.loc.gov/2024056607
LC ebook record available at https://lccn.loc.gov/2024056608

Originally delivered by fleets of horse-drawn wagons, the affordable paperbacks from D. L. Moody's publishing house resourced the church and served everyday people. Now, after more than 125 years of publishing and ministry, Moody Publishers' mission remains the same—even if our delivery systems have changed a bit. For more information on other books (and resources) created from a biblical perspective, go to www.moodypublishers.com or write to:

Moody Publishers
820 N. LaSalle Boulevard
Chicago, IL 60610

1 3 5 7 9 10 8 6 4 2

*Printed in Colombia*

Dedicated to my mom, Muriel, and my dad, Patrick.
God determined before the foundation of the world
to place me in your lives as your daughter. I'll always be
grateful for having you as my parents. Thank you for pointing
me to Jesus and raising me to love and follow Him!
I love you acres and oceans and buckets and barrels full!

# CONTENTS

## STEADFAST SPIRIT

# the next *60 days*

All I ever wanted was to be a mom. On cold winter nights in Southern California where I grew up, I'd snuggle under the covers of my bed and, before drifting off to sleep, pray for my future children while still a child myself. The church community where I grew up placed a high value on motherhood. Many of the homes of my friends from church felt harmonious and happy. My own childhood was filled with plenty of warmth and nurture, but also a fair share of chaos and dysfunction. I pictured my future home encapsulating all of the good, none of the bad.

*And then I had children!*

Along with the blessings, my deep frustrations and even anger *comingled.* To say I felt overwhelmed is an understatement. I wanted to be a triumphant mom, but too often I was triggered. I swore I'd never raise my voice or roll my eyes, but there I was, head hanging low after doing the things I said I'd never do. So, on top of my frustration with my kids, I could barely face my frustration with myself. I wondered, *What must my heavenly Father think of me?*

Can you relate? Are you weary and frustrated with your kids . . . with yourself? Do you want to draw closer to God but feel that because you're an angry and overwhelmed parent, He must be angry with you too?

Marriage and family came much later in life than I anticipated, but with great joy. Perhaps, like me, you can relate to those feelings of wonder as you marvel at the plus sign on a pregnancy test, or when you answer the phone with nervous excitement and hear that the baby you have prayed for is waiting for you at the hospital, ready to meet you and join your forever home. For me, knowing I was going to be a mom was a dream come true! An answer to decades of prayers, the fruition of girlish hopes and longings realized.

When my firstborn son, Oliver, was born, I knew I'd be a great mom. As a capable former nanny and accomplished teacher for nearly a decade, I knew how to run a tight ship with grace and love. I wasn't prepared for the sleepless nights, the colic, the unknowns that turned this woman who likes stability into a fragile worrier. So much of parenting felt confusing and hard. I wondered how in the world anybody in their right mind let us take this beautiful newborn boy home with us in the first place. I second-guessed most of my decisions in those early years and I've learned—now that I have been a mom for seventeen years and counting—that every age and stage of parenting will bring with it new triggers and frustrations, uncertain waters that seem to have no nautical chart to lead the way. Yet, parenting opens up a sea of opportunities for deep spiritual growth and oceans of joy.

When the uncertainties of parenting trouble our hearts, we can allow the sureties of God's Word to soothe them. Psalm 127:3–5a says:

> Children are a gift from the LORD;
> they are a reward from him.
> Children born to a young man
> are like arrows in a warrior's hands.
> How joyful is the man whose quiver is full of them!

As my young children approach adulthood, I'm certain that being a mom is a gift and that the foundation for every transformation is allowing God's Word to soak into our souls—for every good and perfect gift is from above (James 1:17). Many years ago, God met me at the foot of the cross where I laid my triggered heart down at His feet, and He set me free from the generational curse of anger that is no match for the God of all generations. *Overwhelm* became a choice, not a condition I had to live with. It changed me. My home. My legacy.

Over the next 60 days, lay down the guilt and shame you may feel over your angry reactions. Approach each day's reading with an open heart, ready to receive God's grace. Feel the comfort of reading the words from someone who has stood in your shoes and walk with me toward hope and renewal.

# peaceful
# *mind*

# slow to *anger*

*Better to be patient than powerful;*
*better to have self-control than to conquer a city.*
PROVERBS 16:32

Anger is in a hurry, demanding immediate attention. The wise mom doesn't get pushed around by it. She stands as a sentinel, guarding against unrighteous urgency to gather her wits about her and make way for calm. Being slow to anger puts us on the fast track to becoming the godly moms we long to be.

It's not that we never have a temper. I found great freedom and release from guilt when I understood the difference between righteous anger and unrighteous anger. When my child sins, I can feel the pain of it without personalizing it. Their sin is not an offense against me. *It's an offense against God,* and that should grieve me on behalf of Him, but it does not have to wound my heart or make me a victim. Jesus paid the price for their sin and for mine, and so my righteous anger is directed at our mutual enemy: Satan. He would have us misdirect it toward our child and spew and stew— but today, he will be disappointed!

Instead, we make room for empathy in our hearts and see our children with compassion. We can retrain our minds to think, "How sad that sin is having its way with him!" or "What a struggle she must endure in her immaturity and youthful fragility, unable to cope with the temptations she faces!" We are moms ready to use the Word of God delicately to lance hardened hearts, not as a dagger to wound. Our words are sweet with godly and gentle corrections. Our anger draws us closer to sanctification instead of being used against us as a temptation to sin. We don't yell or narrow our eyes in anger. Nor do we say things we'd later regret. What a paradox! Our righteous anger becomes an opportunity for good and one more blessing of stewardship in the high honor of being a mother. Greater than a warrior, indeed. Untriggered and unapologetic—yes, unhurried and unharried—strong in self-control and sanctified in the process.

Lord, it's so easy to take my child's sin or immaturity personally. I know that they don't always have the spiritual maturity to manage their emotions well. Help me model it for them because I love them. I long for them to grow spiritually and to be an example to them. Forgive me for being quick to anger. Help me have compassion on my child when they are rebellious or disobedient. I want to be like that warrior, protecting the walls of my child's heart, not breaking them down with my own hurtful daggers. Thank You, Lord, for empowering me with the ability to direct my anger toward our real enemy and to be the self-controlled mom I long to be. In Jesus' name, amen.

## PUT IT INTO PRACTICE

Even grown women struggle to learn a lesson if we are in a state of high emotion. It's unreasonable for us to think our immature child can either. The next time you are triggered, take a "holy pause" and get your emotions under control. Not everything has to be dealt with right away. Stop. Breathe. Challenge your urgency, and then make a calm and kind choice to speak the truth in love. Do so at a later time when both parent and child are more receptive.

# overwhelm is a *choice*

*He who did not spare his own Son, but gave him up for us all—*
*how will he not also, along with him, graciously give us all things?*
ROMANS 8:32 NIV

It is utterly remarkable that God didn't wait for us to be worthy of His best gifts before giving them to us. In His sacrificial love, He gives us unconditional and limitless supernatural blessings for our human condition. That's good news for triggered moms!

When my first three sons were under four years old, I didn't know how other moms did it. It felt like they had an unspoken guidebook they were following and that somewhere along the way, I wasn't given a copy. My two-year-old was spreading sticky diaper cream all over my one decent armchair when I was busy nursing his baby brother. I couldn't figure out what type of early learning classes were best for my preschooler, and I often felt like crying when I walked the neighborhood with my double stroller, lonely and praying I'd run into someone—anyone—who would engage me in adult conversation. Years later, I felt guilty for letting my teens have too much screen time, or for not making a better effort to schedule time for driving lessons.

Overwhelm has been an unwelcome but constant companion. I felt inferior and ashamed that I wasn't living up to my expectations of the kind of mom I thought I would be. I knew the Bible says that God would never leave me nor forsake me (Hebrews 13:5), but I allowed the demands of my duties to drown out the delights of my devotion to Him. That's when I recommitted to daily devotional time with Jesus: confessing, connecting, and conditioning my heart to receive new mercies. God used lonely parenting seasons where I felt disconnected from others to connect more deeply with Him.

Momma, overwhelm is a choice. Decide that you will not allow it to sabotage your good intentions to meditate on God's Word.

If we truly knew the breadth of His willingness to bless us, we *would* be overwhelmed. Reading our Bibles and devoting this time to Him awakens us to living life to the full—especially when our hands are full! If you choose to be overwhelmed today, choose wisely. Let's be overwhelmed by God's love, not our triggers. God's grace. Not our responsibilities. God's abundance. Not our scarcity. God's strength. Not our weaknesses. Not our failures. *Certainly not our anger.* Let's be overwhelmed in all the best ways.

Lord, I don't want to be overwhelmed by my kids or my triggers. I want to be overwhelmed by the love You offer me. You are generous! Help me receive Your grace. I know that it would be easy for me to feel deep shame and guilt, but if I hold on to those things, Your great sacrifice would be for nothing. I don't want that! I open my heart to Your unconditional love and forgiveness. Thank You, Jesus, for giving Your life for me on the cross. Wash me and cleanse my heart and mind so that I can live my life for You. You tell me that if I believe in You, I will be saved. I believe. Help me to pass on that same love to my children. In Jesus' name, amen.

## PUT IT INTO PRACTICE

Write down three things that overwhelm you in this season of parenting. Next to each one, write a short prayer, asking God for what you need. Now choose a graphic, meme, or a Bible verse that will help you to remember God's overwhelming love and willingness to give you good gifts. Position it where you can see it often. Use it as a screensaver or write it on your bathroom mirror, for example.

# one *trigger* at a time

*Then the righteous will shine like the sun in their Father's Kingdom.*
MATTHEW 13:43

Parenting sometimes feels like sludging through mud. Progress can come so very slowly when we're working on behavior issues with our children. Each step takes great effort, and even though we are headed in the right direction, as soon as we are freed from one sticky situation, we get sucked into another. We long for high ideals, stepping fluidly from one steady stone of progress to another as we help our kids mature. We aim for the stars, imagining our ideal home as we foster a Christ-centered environment—but the reality is we can barely get our teen out of bed on the weekend. All our lofty ideals are bruised as they run up against our triggers.

Don't lose heart, Momma. You don't have to figure it all out today. There may be several areas you want to work on with your kids. Maybe you are triggered by running late everywhere you go. Perhaps you have a houseful of "collectors" and you long for a simplified space free from clutter. Or maybe the overarching tone in your home is grumpy and everyone needs an attitude adjustment. There's no need to tackle it all at once. Pick one trigger that frustrates you the most and set to work, little by little, prayer by earnest prayer, and trust that God will begin to set your feet on a solid path toward progress. Let it take as long as it takes but be consistent—especially in hope!

It's a great comfort to know that this life is a journey, not our final destination. We are sojourners passing through. God promises that there will come a day when those who believe in Him will "shine like the sun in their Father's Kingdom." He's at work *in you*. He's at work *in your child*. There may be only the tiniest spark of optimism, but with the oxygen of wise and loving words in your home, the ember of hope grows. The day you shine like the sun is in your future! Even now, it is reflected in our lives and through the small victories of today. That's a comfort when we can't see through our clouded emotions. Do what you can today and look forward to the completion of the good work that God is starting in you and your home.

> Lord, I know that one day my angry reactions to my triggers will be a thing of the past. I don't want my frustrations to cloud the hope available to me. I trust You to help me shine, in my own small way, in the halls of my home as You renew the halls of my heart with Your power and love. I trust You to complete the good work You have begun. I choose to focus on the next right thing, one trigger at a time. Thank You for giving me hope! In Jesus' name, amen.

## PUT IT INTO PRACTICE

Make a list of the top three things that trigger anger or frustration for you. Now arrange them in order of importance. Beside the #1 trigger, write a verse that will encourage you to be persistent in exchanging your angry reactions for more Christ-centered responses. Next, consider a practical way you can work on this change when you are triggered and practice it daily.

# God grants our *desires*

*Take delight in the LORD,*
*and he will give you the desires of your heart.*
PSALM 37:4 NIV

Of all the desires of my heart as a mom, I wanted my children to be united in the spirit of brotherhood, so Guy and I began with their names: Oliver, Quinn, Oakley, and Quade. Each of their first initials (O, Q, O, Q) are meant to interlock with one another similar to the Olympic symbol. It's a reminder of their bond as siblings and to never let anything break it.

Guy and I share a mutual desire to create strong family ties bound together by godly love. Our hope and prayer is that our boys would always delight in one another—and in God—and that they would admire and respect each other instead of being jealous or mean-spirited. In a world where it's easy to feel contempt and to walk away from one another, we sought to teach them to lean in during hard times instead. Even now, we pray they have unconditional Christlike love for one another, but our intentionality as parents began with lists of baby names as we dreamed about how God would form them uniquely into our family.

Fast-forward to today with two high schoolers, one middle schooler, and a little one in the early years of elementary school. Our boys are great friends with one another, and they talk about living on the same street when they have families of their own, or even going into business together. Even now, they serve alongside one another at church and at school. Although they have a wide age gap between them, we see evidence that God has given us the desire of our hearts. We never know what the results will be when we raise our kids because they will make their own choices, but let's not underestimate the power of prayer and the truth that even when we mess up, God is there to guide and shape our child. He knows that our hearts are often mixed up by sin or ignorance, and yet not even our own human weaknesses can sabotage God's best for our families.

I love the picture of Jesus' mother in Acts 1:14, after He ascended to heaven. The verse says: "They all met together and were constantly united in prayer, along with Mary the mother of Jesus, several other women, and the brothers of Jesus." Though her Son was no longer physically present, I'm sure Mary and Jesus' brothers felt His nearness as they prayed. They delighted in Him and continued to present to Him the desires of their hearts in prayer. What do you desire for your own children? During hard seasons of parenting, it's easy to stop dreaming and praying that God would give us what we desire for our kids. God doesn't give us desires in our hearts just to mess with our heads. Be patient, Momma. Know that the Lord purifies and honors our hearts' desires in His way and in His time.

> God, I know You promise that when I delight in You, you give me the desires of my heart. What I long for most is _____. Lord, I do delight in You. I'm overwhelmed by the thought that You did not only die for me, but You also give me blessing upon blessing. It amazes me that You take delight in me, Your child. I enjoy being in Your presence, and I am grateful that my heart's desires are safe with you. I know that as I spend time with You my desires will be conformed to match Your desires. Thank you for being a generous giver of good gifts. In Jesus' name, amen.

## PUT IT INTO PRACTICE

Do you feel disqualified from receiving the desires of your heart because you feel guilt over your parenting? Begin there. Ask God to help you delight in Him instead of avoiding Him because you feel shame. Take time to talk with your spouse or a trusted friend about what you desire most for yourself as a mom and for your child. Ask them to pray with you that God will give you the desires of your heart as you delight in Him.

# stability during *conflict*

*If your law had not been my delight,*
*I would have perished in my affliction.*
*I will never forget your precepts,*
*for by them you have preserved my life.*
PSALM 119:92–93 NIV

Do you ever feel like nothing is going your way? That even the traffic lights are working against you? Or circumstances feel like wind in your face, stinging your chapped lips and bringing tears to your eyes, forcing your steps backward, try as you might to move forward? As if they have a radar to locate us at our weakest moments, our children push our hot buttons, and we snap! For a little while, we feel justified. But soon we feel like failures, and like the world is failing us too.

Dismay is the opposite of delight, isn't it? It's hard to mask annoyance. But delight? It's equally hard to conceal. I once met a woman at my church's Bible study who oozed with a delight in the Lord. It emanated from her smile, her open body language, the obvious interest in the people around her, and her willingness to serve others. She . . . *glowed.*

Later, as we formed into small prayer groups, I found out that she was experiencing ongoing car trouble and a recent job loss, all while caring for a chronically ill husband and young child. I was amazed. You'd never know that so many hard things were stacked against her. It wasn't because she clammed up and kept things private. Nor was she lamenting her woes to anyone who would listen. She peacefully walked the thorny road she was on with joy that stemmed from a deep love for the promises of God in her most challenging stages of life.

Perhaps this is one of the hardest chapters of *your* life right now. No doubt many of us are recently coming out of one. Momma, God's Word acts as a barrier against the assaults of the world. When nothing makes sense, it is by standing firmly on the truth in Scripture that becomes our delight—not the resolution of conflicts alone. The Lord promises us that He will give us a way of escape when we are tempted (1 Corinthians 10:13), that He has forgiven all our sins (1 John 1:9), that He is our Provider (Philippians 4:19), and that He will guide us in the right direction in our parenting (Psalm 37:23).

When we delight in the Lord, His Word, and in the blessings of our lives, God's goodness overshadows our gloom. It's not that we won't have dark moments of the soul, but they do not have to darken our outlook. One of the greatest kindnesses we can do for our children is to shield them from *our storms* instead of showering them in our stress and anxiety. Let's not allow a child's test of our patience to set off an adult temper tantrum.

Remember the Lord's faithfulness to you personally and be encouraged that no matter what seeks to steal your joy, it cannot steal your Jesus or His resemblance in you unless you let it.

Lord, I want to reflect You when the waters are smooth and when storms churn the waves of life all around me. Bring to my mind the exact Bible verses I need to meditate on when I feel deeply troubled. I praise You when everything is working out and when nothing is easy. Help me be a mom who delights in You and therefore delights in her children in every season. Shield them from the troubles that plague me and help me find my joy in You, not in my circumstances. In Jesus' name, amen.

## PUT IT INTO PRACTICE

The next time your child does something that annoys you, hold your tongue from trying to teach them a lesson when you are emotionally unstable. Pause and think about one thing that you delight in about them. Tell them so and then say a prayer of thanksgiving over them, aloud.

# He knows our *weaknesses*

*He has removed our sins as far from us*
*as the east is from the west.*
*The LORD is like a father to his children,*
*tender and compassionate to those who fear him.*
*For he knows how weak we are;*
*he remembers we are only dust.*

PSALM 103:12–14

There's immense pressure to get everything right in our parenting. We are supposed to have all the answers and make wise decisions. If we fall short of being a model parent, the constant ache in our soul throbs with misery. While it often looked like I was angry with my kids, I was mostly angry with myself.

I'd start my day with sweet words and try to do better. As the day went on, it became harder to *keep calm and carry on*. The patterns seemed set. Unchangeable. It even made me question why God gave me these children in the first place. Maybe I didn't deserve them. Gently, the Lord reminded me that my children are a gift (Psalm 127:3). I don't deserve them! But it is my privilege to delight in them.

Recently, I noticed that there are certain times of day when my teenagers are most likely to trigger me. Armed with this realization, I set out to battle *for them* instead of *against them*. My weapons are praise for the gift of motherhood and compassion for their developing brains that are under a firestorm of hormonal upheaval. Remembering their current weaknesses gives me the strength I needed to give them grace—and a few appropriate recommendations for honorable communication. *Ahem.* Owning our weaknesses as moms frees us to release our kids from paying for theirs.

Mom, in your worst parenting moments, you are still a child of God. Unlike us, He actually does have all the answers and is relentless in His tenderness and compassion for us. We may place a high standard on ourselves, and certainly God calls us to imitate Him in His holiness, but He also "knows how weak we are" and that we need Him to both forgive and guide. Give yourself some of the grace God freely offers to you. Instead of seeking perfection, yield your heart to the process of being perfected in Christ.

> Lord, thank You for reminding me that I'm simply human. I don't want that to be an excuse for sinful behavior, but I am comforted that You are compassionate toward me when I mess up. I don't want to justify my sin or my weaknesses. Lord, give me a tender heart like Yours— both for myself and my children. Help me remember that my child is "but dust" as well and that You will help me grow in compassion for him/her. I praise You for giving me my child. I know he/she is a gift! In Jesus' name, amen.

## PUT IT INTO PRACTICE

The next time you feel frustrated by your sin or weakness, confess it to your child. That's right. It's okay to let them see you struggle and acknowledge when you do wrong. Tell them in an age-appropriate way that you sin too, but that you know the Lord still loves you and will help you. Encourage them that God will help them too.

# less worry, more *prayer*

*Don't worry about anything; instead, pray about everything.*
*Tell God what you need, and thank him for all he has done.*
PHILIPPIANS 4:6

My son Oakley came to the breakfast table and showed me his hand. Two days prior, he had jabbed his palm with a stick while on a field trip to a local bog where his class was inspecting organisms, and soon enough there were unpleasant signs of infection. *I was worried.* Little did I know he would have a freak accident at the playground later that day requiring sixteen stitches in his leg. Suddenly, the splinter in his hand felt less pressing—and far less worrying!

As Oakley lay on the table in urgent care, he endured multiple rounds of shots to numb his leg. The pain was excruciating! Helpless, I grieved for him, and all I could do was hold him tightly, shield his eyes from the doctor's needles, and pray. *And pray and plead, I did!*

After midnight, we made it home from the hospital, tired, but well cared for. As I woke the next morning, I spent time thanking God for all things that went right when it seemed like everything was going wrong. Oakley was incredibly brave during the procedures with the doctors. We came home to a warm bed. Neighbors loaned us crutches. The other boys had stepped up to take care of our youngest son so both my husband and I could go to urgent care. God was providing and taking care of our sweet Oakley.

It's in our human nature to allow worry and fear to turn us manic and reactionary. What happens to you when you are surprised by a calamity?

Once the storm has passed, do you take time to recount the goodness of God? I know that there have been many times when I did not pass the stress test in worrisome moments with my children, but the more we adopt gentle biblical mindsets, the more we will respond with trust and thanksgiving when things don't go the way we planned. When God says not to worry about "anything," it's an invitation to take "everything" that threatens our peace to Him.

It would have been easy and even natural to stew and fret over the multiple medical issues our sweet son was facing. We were certainly feeling our own measure of pain over our son's suffering. None of the worrying would have benefited me, however. When circumstances feel unruly, it's easy to let our emotions go haywire too. Momma, you can be calm and confident today. Do not be afraid. Do not worry. Pray. Ask God for what you need and want. Do it with gratitude for all that He has done and will do for you and your children.

Lord, it feels sickening to worry about my child. I know You have given me a protective mother's heart, but teach me to trust You when my son or daughter is facing trouble of all kinds. Whenever I allow my fear to take over my mind, things just get worse. I want to be a strong and gentle place for my child to rest when stressful moments plague us. Thank You, Jesus, for holding us together when our lives unravel. Recall to my mind all the ways You have helped us before and give us peace. In Jesus' name, amen.

## PUT IT INTO PRACTICE

Describe the ideal response you would want to have in moments of crisis. What Bible verse would be appropriate for you to memorize as your "go-to" passage for when you are worried about your child? Write it out and invite your child to learn it with you.

# a *clean* slate

*This means that anyone who belongs to Christ has become a new person.*
*The old life is gone; a new life has begun!*
2 CORINTHIANS 5:17

I remember walking down the aisles of a big-box grocery store in town years ago. My four-year-old was in the seat of the cart while I wore two different baby wraps—one on the back with my toddler and one on my front with my infant. It was a bit of a spectacle managing three little ones and a basket full of groceries! I remember two things about this season: one, I loved the maternal feeling I had as I held them close. And two, the total frustration that overcame me when I tried to quickly unload my car at home while everything was melting down—the groceries *and* my kids. It amazed me how quickly I could shift from feeling empowered and happy to helpless and disgruntled. And as soon as my temper got the best of me, the best of me was nowhere in sight.

God designed us with an incredible ability to hold on to memories. That's all well and good when they conjure pleasant moments and happy occasions, but when we think back on all the times we said the wrong thing or became sinful in our anger, memories turn from blessings into burdens.

You may not feel like a new creation at this moment. In fact, you may have already lost your cool and snapped at your kids today. When we invite Jesus into our hearts and He wipes our slates clean, our memories are not erased along with our sins. As we fall asleep, flashbacks of how we yelled at our teen for losing her phone at the beach keep us from peaceful rest. The somber, saddened faces of our kids keep coming back to us after an argument with our spouse, even though we swore we'd stop fighting in front of them. We can't change the past, but Momma, you can embrace the truth that Jesus desires to give you a new life in this season of motherhood.

Go back to your childlike devotion to the Lord, and as you draw near to Him, let your actions reflect His transforming power. We have a choice to make each time we are triggered. Will we default to the woman who is dead and gone, or devote ourselves to the new woman God says we are? Your identity as an angry mom is fading into the past, day by day. The events of yesterday are behind you. Out with the old. In with the new. If God sees who we have become, maybe it's time we did too.

Lord, thank You for promising that I am a new person the moment I put my faith in You. Honestly, I don't always feel like I am new because I keep going back to my old, angry ways. I want to respond to my triggers in new ways that reflect the new me. Please stop me in the moment when I begin to revert to the past or when I am triggered. I don't want to contradict who You say I am. I feel hopeful when I consider that my new life in You has already begun, and I look forward to the future instead of being haunted by my past. Give me wisdom and ideas that will bless my children as I parent them that reflect the image of You in my life. In Jesus' name, amen.

## PUT IT INTO PRACTICE

Have you ever been in a car that is brand-new? Then you know that "new car smell." When we belong to Christ, we don't smell any different, obviously! But how can our kids detect that we are, indeed, new creations? Are we giving off an "aroma" of grace? Gentleness? Kindness? Take three minutes to jot down one way your kids benefit from the godly responses and behaviors you demonstrate toward them and then thank the Lord for His transformation in your life.

# is peace *possible?*

*I have told you these things, so that in me you may have peace.*
*In this world you will have trouble. But take heart! I have overcome*
*the world.*

JOHN 16:33 NIV

True peace is not the absence of conflict, it's a condition of our heart. Jesus is the Prince of Peace, and we are adopted into His royal family (Ephesians 1:5). That means godly peace is in our spiritual DNA! Momma, you were designed by a peace-filled God who longs for you to experience His peace routinely—even if your daily routine feels chaotic and hard right now.

In the early years of parenting, I thought one blissful moment would lead to the next. And there have been many! In motherhood, we have lots of opportunities to feel like all is right in the world. We feel it when we see the dimple in our toddler's cheeks. We experience it when they take their first step or their first solo drive around the block. Peace and joy mingle in our hearts when they come to us for morning cuddles or advice on handling friendships. These are the moments that make motherhood so very worth it—and yet, parenting also brings much heartache, doesn't it?

Harmony is not constant in our world and discord strikes when we least expect it. There will be bullies in the schoolyard to deal with, strange illnesses that bring suffering we wish we could remove from our child, feelings of inadequacy as we discover the different needs of each child's unique personality. There will be muddy floors and muddier swamps of confusion along the journey as we face unknowns. And when our kids talk back to us or say things that hurt our feelings? Peace flies right out the finger-smudged window.

If our expectation is that the absence of conflict is peace, we will always operate in turmoil. What if instead of imagining a trigger-free life, we embraced the truth that our peace is in the presence of Jesus, not in the absence of problems? Each time our child walks past the overflowing trash can instead of emptying it or dissolves into tears when we tell them they can't have an ice cream cone, we are not caught off guard. We don't wallow in personal pain or indignation. Our response to our child's drama is not to match it with our own, but to overshadow it with calm, loving correction rooted in the peace of Jesus.

> Dear Jesus, I know you told us that we would have trouble, but I keep being surprised by it. I want to trust that I can overcome these parenting problems through You! Help me have peace in the middle of my troubles and focus on Your promises for me. You don't want me to feel burdened. I thank You for always being my example of victory and for giving me victory in my mind and heart! I choose to believe that You will see me safely through this current trial. In Jesus' name, amen.

## PUT IT INTO PRACTICE

Sometimes, we allow today's trouble to block out all the things we are already having victory over in our parenting. Take five minutes to remind yourself of past troubles that worked out okay. Imagine a symbol that represents the way you were able to overcome that trouble in your past. For example, if you had a child who would not clean their room but eventually you were able to coach them and help them grow in this area, your symbol may be a shirt hanger. Now take that symbol and draw it or use artistic lettering to draw the word. Turn back to this symbol or artistic image whenever you are tempted to think that you are not an overcomer.

# choose your *attitude*

*Sin is no longer your master, for you no longer live under the require-
ments of the law. Instead, you live under the freedom of God's grace.*
ROMANS 6:14

Sometimes we get stuck in the idea that our everyday lives feel unfair.
We wake up early to make breakfast, toss laundry into the dryer, sign papers
for school, scrounge up change for field trip fees, and spend precious minutes searching for shoes that match. Maybe our kids are great around the
house and well-coached to pitch in, but even then, moms will always be the
ones to get things done.

Although God has refined my heart profoundly, I still fight against
bouts of resentment when duties increase. Entitlement creeps in. Thoughts
like *nobody appreciates me!* waft through my mind. My shoulders cramp
and my face tenses when my people are not cooperating. I want them to
acknowledge how their misbehavior affects me! As my attitude teeters on
being testy, I forget that I'm the recipient of what I do not deserve. God's
grace is a gift—no strings attached. I'm not required to acknowledge how
much He has done for me to receive it, but my benefits increase when I do.

It's not only the workload and lack of appreciation that unravels us.
It's our desire that our child conform to us and our way of doing things
more than our desire that they conform to Christ. What if our introverted
selves stopped being frustrated by our extroverted child? How might things
change if we accepted that our daughter's personality doesn't value neatness
like we do? Or that our son's tendency to linger over their dinner plate isn't

meant to annoy us? What if we viewed our child's constant questions as an adorable quirk instead of an annoyance?

Momma, we may need to help our child value alone time or teach them to put socks in the right drawer. Their chilled-out approach to everyday living may be a needed reminder to stop and smell the roses more often. And I promise you that there will come a day when we wished they were there to pelt us with their inquiries.

We are free to choose our attitudes under the grace God has given us. When the demands of motherhood press in, we do not need to become demanding. If we don't like being taken advantage of, we must not take advantage of God's grace either. Use the freedom your faith provides to become the kind of mom who lovingly serves her family, and does so freely from a place of gratitude.

> Lord, I know that You don't force me to do any kind of good work to receive Your love, and yet I often get angry when my kids misbehave or when I feel like I'm doing more than my fair share. I feel unappreciated sometimes. Nor do I value their unique personalities and bent of nature enough. Help me release those feelings. I want to overflow with godly grace. Thank You for freedom to choose my attitude. Thank You for reminding me that the good work I do is never in vain. It's evidence of how grateful I am for You, God. Let me see my child with eyes of joy that You made them in Your image and that we can enjoy our differences. In Jesus' name, amen.

## PUT IT INTO PRACTICE

Do something unexpectedly lavish for your child today that would seem indulgent to them. Say yes to a play date or an extra twenty minutes of playing a game together. Explain to them that God is a generous God who often gives us what we do not deserve because He loves us—and that we do too.

# when you *dread* the future

*So don't worry about tomorrow, for tomorrow will bring its own worries. Today's trouble is enough for today.*
MATTHEW 6:34

The thing about tomorrow is it comes so quickly that it's easy to worry about it today. When I live out tomorrow in my imagination, any and every possible scenario can unfold because the options are endless. During seasons of stress, the imagined future is colored by our worries and anxieties. We don't consider all the good things God has planned. Our default is to dread instead of dream.

Sometimes, today's frustrations are layered by the negativity and fears of tomorrow until the weight of it creates stress that begs for release. You are "fine." And "everything is fine" until your child refuses to buckle their seat belt or your daughter accidentally breaks your favorite plate—the one with the tiny pink roses on it that remind you of your grandmother—and that's it! You overreact and obliterate the normalcy of the moment with your loud voice and piercing glare. The worst thing we can imagine didn't come close, but our reaction to the fairly small offense reveals what we have bottled up inside.

It's not always an explosion of frustration toward our kids. Often, it's the silent stress we carry internally that hampers our parenting—and our well-being. Whenever we are not well emotionally, physically, or spiritually, our kids pick up on it. They feel it. Even the dog feels it. So does the cat! It's true what they say: Momma sets the tone, and when we worry about the future, our mood is electrified with fear and the jolting waves of our anxiety are felt by anyone in close range.

Let me ask you this: Has your mind recently conjured scenes of car trouble, your husband coming home early from work to tell you he's been fired, bullies messing with your son on the playground, or visiting the doctor with your daughter and discovering she has a rare disease, even though you don't have any evidence that those things will ever happen? Me too. It's what moms often do. *But what if we didn't?*

Tension from worry creates vulnerability. Vulnerability makes us susceptible to quick reactions instead of gentle responses. We are on edge. We hold our breath. The slightest trigger tips us over the edge from calm to chaos. Momma, take heart. In Christ, we are secure. There is nothing about tomorrow that can be lived out today. The boundaries of time work in our favor to be present and peaceful, *today.* Moreover, God's strength leads us into tomorrow. Yes, I know. God tells us we will have "issues" related to trials and sorrows. *So. Many. Issues.* But He also reassures us in John 16:33 that we "have peace in" Him. He has overcome the world. None of its troubles need to trouble us because He has "overcome the world." It's true for today. It will still be true tomorrow.

Heavenly Father, You have everything in control and I don't need to worry about tomorrow. Thank You for reassuring me that I do not need to worry. I don't want to feel on edge or fearful. Relieve my anxiety so that I can be more fully present, calm, and kind. I know that as my good Father, You have good plans for me and my children. Right now, I release my dread, and I trust You to handle all my issues that make me nervous and edgy. Thank You for your peace. I receive it. In Jesus' name, amen.

## PUT IT INTO PRACTICE

The opposite of dread is dreaming. Let's do that together for a moment. What's one desire God has put on your heart for your children? What's one dream you have for your role as a mother? For good measure, what's a personal dream you have for your life that is not related to motherhood? Write down one practical step you can take to put that dream into motion.

# picture-perfect
# *parenting?*

*When he saw the crowds, he had compassion on them because they
were confused and helpless, like sheep without a shepherd.*
MATTHEW 9:36

"You never believe me!" my friend's daughter shouted at her mom.
Our kids were hanging out together at a park when Anne's younger brother
Marty found their mom so he could tattle, accusing Anne of hitting him
in the head with a volleyball "on purpose!" All too aware that we were in
public with other parents watching, my friend took Marty at his word. In
an attempt to save face rather than allow a scene to develop, she quickly
dismissed Anne's protests. Frustration welled up and out of her twelve-year-
old, who clearly had a different version of what had happened on the volleyball court where a group of girls had been playing a friendly game together.

I could see the slump in my friend's shoulders as the drama unfolded.
She felt like she couldn't win because the truth from one child was being
hotly challenged by the other. The volleying of "she said-he said," led to
confusion and a blanket timeout for both accusing children. Nobody was
winning on the volleyball court or in the court of family feud.

Instinctively, I hugged my friend in sympathy. Nobody likes to have
their kids argue in public or say things that put us in an unpleasant light.
It's embarrassing! One of my desires as a mom who struggled with being
triggered myself was to normalize the fact that we all struggle and that

nobody's kids are perfect. No mom gets it right all the time. No family with multiple children lives in constant harmony.

What if we move toward empathy and away from judgment when our mom friends share their guilty feelings or worst mom moments? Or how about this: what if you gave yourself grace for the times when you felt caught between a rock and a hardheaded teen or preschooler? Matthew 9:36 gives us a glimpse of Jesus' heart for us in our confusion and helplessness—He has "compassion" on us! Not condemnation.

It's okay to admit we don't know what to do, even right there in the middle of the argument. Instead, we can offer compassion, saying, "I'm not totally clear about what happened. I do know you are both upset, and I care. Let's take a breather and I promise to help you work through this problem in a little bit." In the meantime, we acknowledge their feelings, soothe sore heads, and give assurance that at the right time, with clear and kind compassion, we will help them learn from their conflicts.

We won't solve every problem or always know the truth when our kids are tangled in tattling. We do get to guide our kids toward honesty and the open-mindedness to see things from another's perspective. Let's let go of our own need to present a perfectly put-together picture of our children. Good parenting isn't a home free from triggers. It's living untriggered in the midst of them. It's showing the patience and kindness of the Holy Spirit in real life moments. A picture of godly grace worth capturing.

Holy Spirit, I want to have a mind that is filled with wisdom and responds with patience when my child is angry or hurt. Fill me with godly counsel. Help me slow down when my son or daughter is in the middle of a crisis or when sibling rivalry is at play. I want to release my need to fix things immediately and instead work on reaching their heart. Thank You for giving me wise insights I wouldn't normally live out. Thank You for helping me cast off my fear of what others will think as I parent in a way that may be different from my peers. Pleasing You is what matters most. In Jesus' name, amen.

## PUT IT INTO PRACTICE

What is your most embarrassing parenting moment? It loses its power when we put it out there. Share it in an appropriate way on social media or with a mom friend. Let them know that you are a work in progress and that even when things don't go as you wish, you are thankful that God gives you grace and helps you learn from these triggered moments.

# when their words *wound*

*A fool is quick-tempered,*
*but a wise person stays calm when insulted.*
PROVERBS 12:16

My child came to me with that look on his face, the one where he was about to ask me for something. It was Sunday afternoon, and I was looking forward to a day of resting after a morning at church. My heart longed for times of quiet to play games, sip iced tea on our southern screened-in porch, and enjoy my children. "Mom, can you take me to the store and then drop me off at Mike's house?" he asked me, already tying the laces of his shoes in expectation.

"Not now, son." I spoke firmly but kindly.

"What?!" he exploded. "Why not? You're so mean, Mom!"

My head whipped up. I felt the switch in my brain flip from calm to calculated as I reviewed all the things I had said yes to over the last two days. I was triggered, but calm.

"Son, you don't get to insult me by saying I am 'mean' to you. I am kind and good and generous to you and I am happy to be that kind of mom. Let me help you remember your blessings. On Friday, I said yes to allowing you to go on a sleepover. On Saturday morning I got up early to go get you from your friend's house. Later that day, I took you to the pool to swim and made you a wonderful lunch. Last night, I allowed you to meet up with your teammates to kick the ball around at the park. Your heart should be over-flowing with gratitude over the kindness and generosity of your mom." My boy softened and then sobered. Quickly, he apologized, and then slipped off his shoes.

I know how to match insult for insult, but when I remember that my immature kids don't keep a record of my generosity, the truth is, I can speak clearly and kindly as I remind them of how blessed they are. My tone makes a difference—to speak with wisdom, not sputter with wild indignation. Momma, which it will be? Will your parenting triggers have an ungodly impact on you, or will you impact your child by your godly responses?

Be encouraged. It takes practice to learn to remain cool when we'd rather be hot-tempered. While God has done a lot of work in my life, I am right there with you. Give yourself permission to grow in this area and develop empathy in exchange for indignation. I've learned that my kids' insults are more about their self-focus than what they really think of me. Resist the temptation to rehearse the hurt. Remaining calm in the face of hot-tempered kids is evidence of God's work in our lives. Each trigger is a distinguishing moment for you and me to model wisdom and promote peace.

> Jesus, I know that on this earth, You were often insulted and yet You handled each accusation and word spoken against You with grace and gentleness. I know You will help me when my kids are offensive or take me for granted. Help me stay calm when I am insulted, whether it's by my kids or someone else. Bring to my mind the truth of who I am in You and let that be enough for me. I know that we all need to focus more on gratitude in our home. Lord, thank You for taking the insults of others for me so that I could live free from condemnation. I love You! In Jesus' name, amen.

## PUT IT INTO PRACTICE

What are your two best qualities as a mom? Take time today to ask your child what they think makes you a good mom. Relish their words and take them to heart. Recall them often!

# when you don't know the way *forward*

*He led me to a place of safety;*
*he rescued me because he delights in me.*
PSALM 18:19

I was panicking. The fear was so strong that I forced myself to remain calm and pray. I didn't want to alarm my sweet children. The kids and I were visiting a pumpkin patch one fall day several years ago. We decided to enter the famous corn maze that stretched across a massive farm field. At first we had fun, weaving and dodging down rows of towering stalks of corn, following the map the farmhands provided. Quade, my fourth son, was a baby, and he kicked his legs happily from the carrier across my torso. But minute by minute, the bewilderment began to set in as each row that we thought would empty us into open fields became another twist or dead end, and it was getting dark.

Strangely, we didn't run into any other guests who might aid us in our escape. The boys were tired. And thirsty. The rows of corn were thick, and breaking through left us scratched and even more lost. Finally, after nearly three hours, we found our way to the end of the labyrinth. I cried with relief, quickly wiping my tears away in embarrassment.

We headed to our car and happily started for home. One by one, each son fell asleep before we made it safely into our driveway. Once inside the house, they were ready for bed. As I tucked them in, I marveled at how

precious they were to me. They had been delightful in a difficult situation. I was proud of them for hanging in there during our maniacal maze.
Though they cried out a time or two that they were hungry or needed
water, they followed me, their momma, down each path ahead without
questioning me, unafraid. They did not know the way, but they trusted me
to make a way. Honestly, I was too focused on escape to even snap at them
or get irritated. Imperfectly, I led them through to completion. It makes me
all the more thankful that our heavenly Father knows exactly where we are
going even when we feel dazed and confused.

We never have to feel lost in motherhood. God would search the whole
earth to find us and take our hands. Are you in your own "twisted maze,"
feeling like you don't know what to do next? Maybe your school choice has
suddenly been blocked or the house you were hoping to live in was sold
to someone else. Perhaps an opportunity you have always wanted is now
being offered to you, but the unknown feels crippling. Our surroundings
are not what we expected and our minds leap to fear or uncertainty. *The
world is at odds with our comfort levels.*

God sees our position from the high places. He sees every angle of the
maze of your life, the roadblocks you are facing with your child's health,
the path you are walking that feels like quicksand. He sees you in your
need for stability when the earth is giving way beneath your feet. Ask Him
for sustenance. Request refreshment. Follow Him, peacefully forward,
even if your legs feel tired and your body weak. Your good Father delights
in you and in leading you forward. God will rescue you from yourself,
your trials, and your triggers. He will usher you forth into safe, open places,
for He delights in you.

**Lord, I trust You to lead me to safekeeping. You see the path before
me and where it leads. You know what is best for my child too. Help
me trust You, knowing you are not just responsible for me, but that**

You delight in me. Give me a peaceful mind as I face the unknown. I want to trust You without fear. Thank You for all the ways You keep me and my family safe that I may never even realize. I know You want what is best for us. In Jesus' name, amen.

## PUT IT INTO PRACTICE

Take the path less traveled around your home or neighborhood, just for today. If you usually walk down the hall to the nearest bathroom, go upstairs instead. Drive the backroads to pick up your groceries. As you go, remember that God sees you and the path you are on at all times. There is joy to be had each step of your day, even if you don't know what is around the corner.

# don't borrow *trouble*

*You are the light of the world—like a city on a hilltop that cannot be hidden. No one lights a lamp and then puts it under a basket. Instead, a lamp is placed on a stand, where it gives light to everyone in the house. In the same way, let your good deeds shine out for all to see, so that everyone will praise your heavenly Father.*

MATTHEW 5:14–16

Two of my four sons are not morning people, and all it takes is one. One gruff grunt. One frown. One rejection of bacon and eggs. That's all it takes to get me defensive. I used to feel dampened by their morning cloud of misery, but they have slowly improved in their wake-up routine, and I have slowly improved in my understanding that their mood has nothing to do with me. Taking it personally was my own problem. Rather than influencing my kids, they were influencing me—and I needed to change my attitude before I began to work on theirs.

Sometimes we borrow the attitudes of others. Instead of allowing our child's fussiness to make us fussy, we can push back the storm clouds with our own sunny outlook. Too often, I allowed my child's triggered state to trigger me. It made no sense for them to have that kind of influence over me when my desire was to be Holy Spirit–influenced, even on early mornings when my boys would rather sleep in.

Shake it off, Momma, like you shake raindrops from an umbrella. Shake off the dreariness and resolve to change the atmosphere in your home when the outlook of others looks dim. It has been said that Momma sets the tone.

When it seems like you are not making a difference, be assured that your peaceful perspective is in fact overshadowing the negativity around you. My kids have often come to me sheepishly apologetic for their morning blunders. Because I didn't meet their complaints with my own, they knew I was a safe harbor for them to approach when the Lord convicted them. Our untriggered responses are rays of gospel light revealing a better course to our children that they will pursue as they mature.

All it takes is one: one mom willing to be a light in her home.

Lord, I know that I often take my kids' attitudes personally and I need to put some healthy perspectives in place. I know that I have the privilege to be a safe harbor for them when their attitudes and moods are a tumultuous mess. Help me be gentle when I deal with their inappropriate words and actions. Show me discernment so I can tell when to discipline them lovingly and when to overlook an offense. Help me be a light in my home, even when my child has a dark cloud hanging over them. I want to set a tone of love and understanding while also showing them that I am here to help them mature. Thank You, Lord, for helping me have wisdom and understanding. In Jesus' name, amen.

## PUT IT INTO PRACTICE

Notice the weather outside today. Describe how the atmosphere—whether rainy or stormy—is all part of the wonder of how God designed the world. What can you appreciate about the rain? The sun? The wind? Practice expressing gratitude for the different seasons and climates. Notice how the trees remain steadfast in every changing season. Imagine yourself as that tree, strong and resilient, unaffected by storms.

# the *myth* of perfection

*What we suffer now is nothing compared to the glory he will reveal to us later.*

ROMANS 8:18

It was a nearly perfect day. Any imperfection was easily overlooked amid the fun our family was having at a local amusement park. We got out of the house on time and without a lot of cajoling and pleading to hurry up. The traffic was light and the crowds low. We got onto roller coasters with ease, and amazingly, the boys were warm and kind to one another, never fretting over who got to ride with whom. All. Day. Long. Even the weather was sunny with a lovely breeze. My husband, Guy, and I marveled at the end of the day that there had been none of the usual squabbles or mishaps. Years later, I often look back on that day, mainly because I can't think of a nearly perfect family day before or since. They are rare in my experience!

So often I've remembered that day with gratitude. It gives me hope that shiny, happy days do exist, even if ever so briefly in the span of our lives. Momma, you may be in an endless season of meeting one need after another, or witnessing sibling rivalry that breaks your heart, or maybe you are wrestling with comparing your life to a friend's, whose home life seems so much more exciting or easy. But that is a myth. Living in a broken and sin-filled world prevents optimal conditions for a perfect life or relationships.

We create myths in our minds and hold on to them as facts. What we see becomes our truth, but it's faith—believing in what we cannot see—that gives us hope. It's a myth that anyone or anything is truly perfect or simple. This isn't meant to discourage us. We never have to succumb to frustration or weariness as Christ-filled mommas. Tap into the strength and refreshment that comes from the Lord. Godly joy and contentment are available to us, even on our most flawed day.

Has there been a season that you can look back on with fondness? As you reflect on the past, allow the joys of yesterday to balance your perspective about today's trials. Then, look to the future, and set your mind on things above, knowing that real perfection—and paradise—awaits!

Lord, most of my days feel challenging and I long for better days. I know that there is goodness to experience even in hard seasons. You have given me a bright future to look forward to! Help me not get caught up in the drama or triggers in my everyday life and give me an eternal perspective. Thank You for giving me glimpses of beauty and peace even when I'm surrounded by moments that trigger me. I look forward to all You have prepared for us in heaven! In Jesus' name, amen.

## PUT IT INTO PRACTICE

At your next meal, ask your child what their idea of a perfect morning would be like. Ask another family member what their best day has been in the last year. Take time to reflect on the goodness of God.

# the *source* of peaceful parenting

*You will keep in perfect peace*
*all who trust in you,*
*all whose thoughts are fixed on you!*
ISAIAH 26:3

When Jesus slept peacefully in the boat in the middle of a storm, His disciples were panicked. Picture the chaos of the waves threatening to capsize the boat and plunge them into the sea. Imagine the relaxed features of Jesus' face as He slept. His friends woke Jesus up soon enough and pleaded with Him to save them! Jesus spoke with authority, and a great calm settled all around them. He even questioned why these men were so afraid (Mark 4:38–40).

Today you may be experiencing a storm in your life. Are there people or circumstances that you can't control, creating drama or problems for you? Our triggered state doesn't always originate because of something our kids are doing. External triggers make us afraid, quick to anger. They worry us to the point that even innocent things our kids do set us off. We overreact and over-discipline because we ... are ... just ... *over* ... it!

Momma, Jesus is in your boat. He knows the storm is raging around you and that your emotions are raging right along with it. He is not caught up in the whirlwind. He is not worried about the circumstances because He knows He is able to give you and me peace in the middle of the storm.

Isaiah 26:3 reminds us that God grants peace, perfect peace, to those who trust in Him and "whose thoughts are fixed" on Him. When you are tempted to forcefully figure out an escape and none is obvious, turn your mind back to Jesus and His peace-filled presence.

As we settle into the gentle arms of God, we see our problems in a better light. Our nerves are soothed and so is our mood. It's a gift to show our kids that even when we have reason to fear, we have a greater reason to trust God and that He will help us in times of need. Our steadiness in the storm is a testimony of Jesus to our children, establishing trust with them in our relationship and cultivating their own hope and trust in God.

Lord, I trust You to keep me in a place of perfect peace in the storms of life. I choose to keep my eyes on You when the waves rise on every side. You can resolve all my concerns. I trust You! Help me be a peaceful mom who treats her child with mature godliness even when times are hard, so that I never take out my fear or worry on him/her. Thank You for being my peace and reminding me I do not need to be afraid. In Jesus' name, amen.

## PUT IT INTO PRACTICE

Take a short walk outside today with your child—even if they are teenagers. Notice nature all around you. Reflect on the truth that Jesus is Lord over it all and let His peace fill your heart. Point out the beauty of the weather, cloudy or sunny, and talk with your child about how God is all-powerful, and that even nature must obey Him.

# let *forgiveness* flow

*Make allowance for each other's faults, and forgive anyone who offends you. Remember, the Lord forgave you, so you must forgive others.*
CoLOSSIANS 3:13

Forgiven. That's your position today. As a kid, I was typically a rule fol-lower. I wanted to do the right thing and mostly kept myself out of trouble. If the teacher told us to line up, I didn't linger. When my dad asked me to be home at a certain time, I complied. So when one of my kids in particular seemed bent on breaking every rule—and looking annoyingly cute while doing it—I was perpetually flabbergasted.

These days, he has matured, and we are working on his occasional im-pulsiveness, which usually rears its head when his buddies come around. Just yesterday, he joined them in throwing gummy worms at spectators sit-ting in the baseball stadium. One sugary treat was launched after another, and soon enough it soured the fun when a little kid got hurt. Sigh. Every stage of parenting has its challenges, doesn't it?

Still, I'm encouraged by this passage from Colossians, which reminds me to "make allowance" for his faults. God asks me, and you, to forgive "any-one" who offends us. As moms, we are perfectly positioned to be offended on a daily basis. The triggers can be so consistent that being defensive and offended becomes *who we are*, not just something *we feel on occasion*. Be-ing annoyed and frustrated becomes a default setting where every day feels hard and all we can see is how our kids are working to trigger us. This faulty mindset magnifies their faults and minimizes our high calling to forgive.

There is no sin that escapes Jesus' grace and no grudge we can hold on to when we grasp it. Forgiveness is a heavenly calling that beckons us to rise above when our child tries to get a rise out of us. It's an attitude of grace and mercy that not only blesses our sons and daughters but reminds us to reflect on how much we too have been forgiven.

> Lord, I don't want to feel resentful. It doesn't feel good to always expect the worst or to live on edge for the next trigger to tear away at my peace. I know You have forgiven me. Thank You! Give me a heart of forgiveness that is quick to make allowances for my child's faults. Help me know that is not permissive parenting, but that I need to be more proactive to work with my child when they struggle. Help me keep doing the good parenting and trust You to work in my child's life. I forgive my child, and I thank You for giving us both grace. In Jesus' name, amen.

## PUT IT INTO PRACTICE

Practice offering words of forgiveness to your child, even if they do not ask for it or apologize. They may not be old enough to do so, or they may simply not have learned to be humble in this way. Model it for them in moments of calm after an offense has occurred, without retelling or lecturing: just simple, unoffended forgiveness.

# staying *present*

*A cheerful heart is good medicine,*
*but a broken spirit saps a person's strength.*
PROVERBS 17:22

It was a happy moment. All four of my sons were sitting on the couch alongside me in our living room on the first day of summer break. A classic sci-fi movie was playing in the background, and we sat comfortably enjoying downtime. In a house full of energetic kids, it was a special departure from the norm of our schedules and our typical rowdy vibes.

Suddenly, my mind wandered. I pondered the fact that I had only one more summer before our oldest child would leave for college. Soon, family movie nights would be a bittersweet memory. I imagined what life would be like when our youngest son, born ten years after his oldest sibling, was the sole child under our roof without the companionship of his older brothers, who would have moved on toward independence. As thoughts bathed in scarcity flooded my mind, I forgot God's abundant goodness. I couldn't focus on the movie, much less the tranquil peace of being together as a family.

It wasn't long before I started feeling restless and my breathing quickened. My heart dropped as sadness crept in. I couldn't leave well enough alone and just be present. I was letting the future—my imagined, lonely future—steal the joy of today. God gives us many happy moments daily. Being intentional to stay in them is a barrier against being triggered, Momma. Fewer things set us off when we embrace the happy occasions in front of us. Personally, when my outlook is sunny, I see the difference it makes in the tone of our home and how the boys interact with me and one another.

Yesterday, I got word that a friend of mine lost her son after his long battle with a childhood illness. Though he is in heaven and her family rejoices that they will be with the Lord and their boy again one day, it's a reminder to embrace every moment with our children. I read through my sweet friend's remembrances of her boy, highlighting their love of camping in the mountains, family game nights, and volunteering at church together. Though she had reason for sorrow, it was her joy during this incredible pain that made me marvel. Even now, her cheerful heart is evident amid her grief, and the strength of the Lord is apparent for all to see as a witness of her faith.

Being thankful for the present is "good medicine." Many of our triggers are battled in our minds. Allowing fear for the future and negativity to creep in weakens our defenses and makes us defensive. Is there something you are worrying about that may or may not turn out like you expect? When God places curves in the road, it's tempting to strain to see around the corner, but then we miss the view right beside us. If you are spending a lot of time in your imagination, you may need to come back down to earth. These sweet moments of bonding are not to be missed. They do our hearts good! Anticipate that more will come, and release the unknowns of tomorrow to God, who lovingly directs your steps.

Lord, I know that You have good plans for me and for my family. I don't know what the future holds, but I spend a lot of time worrying about it. I'm missing out on the here and now. You never let us down! Help me cherish the happy moments—and even the hard ones too as I look for how You will bring good from them. You have purposely designed for us to enjoy today. When I worry about what might happen to my kids or where we will be living next year, or what friendships they will form, I can feel the weakness of my soul. I want to be strong in You instead. Help me, Lord! I look forward to being more present and mindful about today's blessings. In Jesus' name, amen.

## PUT IT INTO PRACTICE

Every time you begin to worry about the future, look down at your shoes. Remind yourself that you are here. Right now! There is nothing more you need to focus on than this moment. Cherish it!

# God keeps His *promises* to you

*The rain and snow come down from the heavens*
*and stay on the ground to water the earth.*
*They cause the grain to grow,*
*producing seed for the farmer*
*and bread for the hungry.*
*It is the same with my word.*
*I send it out, and it always produces fruit.*
*It will accomplish all I want it to,*
*and it will prosper everywhere I send it.*
Isaiah 55:10–11

There are over 8,000 promises in the Bible. The promise that the Word of God prospers wherever God sends it is especially comforting. When the Holy Spirit convicts us for our quick tempers, there are two things to consider: First, we are fully equipped by the Holy Spirit to hold our tongues and speak kindly even if our child is unkind (2 Peter 1:3). And second, Isaiah 55:10–11 promises that God will bring fruit from His Word in His time, not ours. The seeds of Scripture I have planted in my child's heart may be sleepy, but they are not dormant.

We blossom because of God's work in us. Like a faithful farmer, the Holy Spirit is dealing with our weeds and testing our soil so that we can prosper spiritually. But let's be frank. Sometimes the manure stinks! God's correction toward us and correcting our kids can be equally messy at times. Decide what kind of harvest you are seeking to produce. What we sow, we reap. Get your fingers dirty. Pray that your child's heart receives the Word and pray for prosperity in his/her spiritual life. Relish the process instead of resisting it. It will sustain, satisfy, and bless your life. What a relief to know that it's not up to us to produce the harvest of good character in our children. God will do it as we steward it.

Momma, we are fully equipped to say what is right and good in the heat of the moment. The seeds of truth that are planted in *us* are ripe with urgency to produce fruit within the soil of *our* hearts. In the same way, the Holy Spirit is at work, right now, to bring your son or daughter to a place of spiritual maturity in due time. Are you willing to keep planting, watering . . . and trusting God as you wait?

As we go into the rest of what is left of this day, reflect on the power of our words to plant blessing and encouragement in the hearts of our children. We can either be used to poison and harm or be a vessel to water and refresh our child's soul with love and encouragement. Let the Holy Spirit uplift you as each challenge presents itself today, knowing that nothing— not even your triggers—can suppress what God has guaranteed.

> Dear God, I can believe Your promises. Thank You for reminding me that I am only required to be faithful to plant Your Word in my heart and to instruct my child toward the truth of Your Word. You do the rest. You promise to make it fruitful. Help me be patient with the process. I know You will do what You say. Help me be expectant and hopeful as I wait and look forward to the harvest. In Jesus' name, amen.

## PUT IT INTO PRACTICE

This week, plant a seed in a small pot of soil. Water it, give it sunshine, and watch it grow day by day. Notice the benefits of faithful nurturing and know that this is true of your child's heart too. Let it be a reminder that God is at work even when we don't see evidence immediately.

# satisfied
*soul*

# embracing the *gift* of parenting

*Pursue righteousness, godliness, faith, love, endurance and gentleness.*
1 TIMOTHY 6:11 NIV

Most days, I'm content to launch into my normal routine, which, let's be honest, can go sideways fast when kids are involved. Just because we are busy parenting doesn't mean we get a free pass from pursuing righteousness or gentleness. Nope. During this season of mothering—making peanut butter and jelly sandwiches, wiping feverish brows, and carpooling kids around—we are called, even then, to pursue spiritual growth. What does that look like when you are knee-deep in diapers or negotiating screentime with your teenager? How do we pursue such lofty things when we can barely keep up with all the demands of everyday parenting challenges?

*The answer is in the attitude.* Insignificant activities in the earthly realm become supernatural pursuits in the spiritual realm if we recognize them as good works God created us in advance to do (Ephesians 2:10).

It'd be easy to slop together a sandwich and sigh over how much work I must do. A normal response to kids clamoring for more video games would be exasperation. I'm sure other moms and dads would knowingly approve if I raised my voice and then shouted louder than I intended when nobody came to the table and the dinner got cold. But what if I spread the jam and spread some joy while I was at it? How might an inquisitive conversation about my child's desire for more screens allow me to show interest in the things that interest them, and convey how very interesting they are to me? What if I take the opportunity to offer loving consequences when kids don't come to the table and use it as a teachable moment instead of exploding in anger?

We won't get parenting right every time, so let's go ahead and remove any unrealistic standards we are striving toward. Still, it's often the little things that make the biggest impact over time. Each time we do the next necessary thing for our kids, we are fulfilling a chance to be the hands and feet of Jesus to them—the gift that keeps on giving!

Pursuing godliness sounds lofty, but it becomes a reality by placing high value on mundane acts of service. Our mothering is missional, a significant pursuit of "righteousness, godliness, faith, love, endurance and gentleness" in all we do.

> Lord, I want to live a life of significance! I often feel like I'm simply going from one task to another, and it can easily overwhelm me. My attitude starts to stink when I feel stretched too thin over thankless duties. Help me see the value in pursuing godliness and gentleness in everything I do as a parent. Give me joy as I seek to put on a better attitude that reflects my love for You and my children, Lord. Help me see the fruit of sowing the seeds of faith into my everyday moments as a mom. Remind me that my kids are watching and learning, and what a high honor it is to be Your hands and feet in serving them. In Jesus' name, amen.

## PUT IT INTO PRACTICE

Name your least favorite task as a parent. What words describe your attitude about it? Flip the script in your head. How can you affirm something good about this situation? What is the vale in it? Write it down. Return to this page where you have written this new script down and review it later today or tomorrow. Do you notice a difference in your attitude as you begin to think more positively about the value of what you do as a mom?

# *good* news

*For this is how God loved the world: He gave his one and only Son, so that everyone who believes in him will not perish but have eternal life.*
JOHN 3:16

Momma, God loves you. Did you read that carefully? *He* loves you. He *loves* you. He loves *you*. Being a mom unearths from the recesses of our hearts the depth of our sacrificial love for our children. Just like God! As a Father, He went to great lengths to show His love to us when he sacrificed His Son, Jesus, on the cross to die for our punishment.

As triggered moms, we know that we have fallen short of God's holy standard. We have sinned and we know it. But that's not where the story ends. Jesus, the perfect Son of God, died to save us from our sin, for every angry reaction and unkind word.

The Bible tells us that if we confess our sins, God will forgive us and cleanse us (1 John 1:9). Have you felt that sin has had a chokehold on you? When we pray, "God, I know that I am a sinner. I confess it. I believe that Jesus died for my sins, and I want Him to be Lord over my life," we no longer face the punishment of our sins! Instead, we are clean and forgiven. In fact, our sins have been removed as far as the east is from the west, and we are seen in God's eyes as clean and forgiven (Psalm 103:12).

Maybe you have never given your life and your heart to God. Your feelings of guilt and shame are continually present. You feel guilty for what you have done. Shame is a feeling about who you are. Jesus offers you freedom from both. He has already paid the price for what you have done, and He has re-created who you are in Him—He sees you as a new person (2 Corinthians 5:17).

Even after we are saved by grace, we still live in a fallen, sinful world. If we continue to struggle with unrighteous anger, we may need to bow at the foot of the cross, look into the loving eyes of Jesus, who willingly laid down His life for us, and return to the joy of our salvation (Psalm 51:12). It's impossible for joy and anger to reside in our hearts at the same time. Let this be your one thing when nothing else is working. Meditate on God's goodness and Jesus' sweeping grace.

Do you yell?

Have you said hurtful things?

Does your heart brim with frustration? And regret?

You are forgiven.

You are loved.

The enemy of our souls wants to overwhelm us with guilt over what we have done and shame us for who we are. But God wiped away his influence over you with Jesus' death on the cross. Each time you are triggered, return to joy and watch as God frees you to live, *un*triggered.

Dear Jesus, thank You for saving me. You took my sins and made me clean and forgiven. I receive Your forgiveness and I praise You for making me a new person. I love You. Nobody has ever loved me like You do. I release this pent-up anger and frustration, and I exchange it for Your joy because of my salvation! From this moment on, I yield my triggers to You. In Jesus' name, amen.

## PUT IT INTO PRACTICE

Did you say the prayer of salvation? If you did, will you email me and let me know? I'd love to pray for you and rejoice with you over how God has transformed your life, as well as offer you other resources to help you in your walk with Jesus. Welcome to the family, Sister! I praise God for you! My email address is: Amber@AmberLia.com.

# releasing *comparison* in your life

*Let the message about Christ, in all its richness, fill your lives. Teach and counsel each other with all the wisdom he gives. Sing psalms and hymns and spiritual songs to God with thankful hearts. And whatever you do or say, do it as a representative of the Lord Jesus, giving thanks through him to God the Father.*

COLOSSIAN 3:16–17

I was working three jobs, homeschooling four little boys, and taking care of my sick parents. Stress was affecting me so severely that I was having trouble breathing normally on most days. I did what I could for relief—long walks, breathing exercises, and lots of prayer helped—but it didn't remove the constant pressure. Self-pity and resentment kept trying to wedge their way into my heart to crowd out peace and joy.

I could come up with plenty of things to be upset about if I let myself. It didn't help when I started scrolling pictures of friends on social media, jetting off to Italy (*ITALY, really?!*) or enjoying picnics in the park. In a nutshell, life felt unfair. One of my biggest triggers was the burden of responsibility, and the other was my self-imposed deadline for the end of my difficulties. In my estimation, the season of suffering had lasted long enough. Comparing my life to others was one thing, but comparing my life to my own expectations was even more defeating.

The thing is, I don't get to tell God when enough is enough. It's not that my hard times were not hard. *They were.* But when my mind plants ideas like, "Amber, you deserve so much better than this" or "Nobody understands how hard or unique your situation is!" it's a sign that I've mistakenly believed that my purpose in life is freedom from trials. Comparing my life to yours, hers, or my own fantasies makes me unsettled, ungrateful, and in danger of coming *unglued.* Becoming untriggered means rising above when we begin to sink low.

Part of God's good will and plan for us is to be moms marked by thanksgiving and gratitude. When you stop and think about it, it's mind-blowing that God wants me and you to represent Jesus here on earth, whether on the outskirts of town *or Italy.* We get to represent the Lord when demands are high, when nobody notices our efforts, and when our families ask more of us than we think we have to give. And when we do, our lives are enriched, our hearts thankful. What flows out of our mouths is praise for all God has done for us—which is beyond comparison!

Lord, I don't want to be mistaken about the blessings all around me, regarding them as burdens. Help me see my life as You do. Comparing my situation to other moms' lives does me no good and only makes me feel worse. Give me a renewed joy and gratitude for my family and my calling to be their mom. Lord, I praise You for all the good gifts You have already given to me! I want to represent You well. Change my perspective so that I don't view other people's lives as easier or better than mine. When I'm resentful, nobody feels good, especially me. Renew a right spirit within me and give me hope and joy as I face each responsibility You have given to me. I love You and I am thankful for this life You have given to me. In Jesus' name, amen.

## PUT IT INTO PRACTICE

What is good about this season you are in now? How can you "represent" Jesus and His lavish gift of salvation and goodness in your home today?

# you don't need to fix it *today*

*For everything there is a season,*
*a time for every activity under heaven.*
ECCLESIASTES 3:1

Every year, I look forward to ordering my new daily planner. I'm one of those overzealous people who gets a kick out of using erasable colored pens to code the varying activities of our lives: blue for the boys' appointments, green for my work meetings, and pink for anything fun or personal, like getting a manicure or a family vacation by the ocean. In a world where digital calendars are popular, I still love turning the sturdy pages of my organizer and putting pen to paper, filling the lines that hold space for the daily activities that make up our lives.

And yet, looking at all the responsibilities ahead also creates stress and anxiety more than I care to admit. It's one thing to be organized and another to be agonized over the day before us. You can almost bet on it: When my day becomes too full, or I look ahead and see a worrisome activity, I can feel my heart begin to pump a little faster and my breath quickening. What starts out as feeling in control by putting everything in its place can quickly become a mental landslide where anxiety engulfs the initial excitement for what's to come. And it doesn't take much. We can be one carpool-scheduling debacle away from feeling frantic.

For me, anxiety and worry are quickly followed by being short-tempered. I lose patience for the child who needs help with finding his team jersey, or with the son who simply wants to share what happened at school yesterday when I'm in the middle of spiralizing zucchini for dinner. Instead of welcoming their needs, I'm irritated by them. It all becomes too much!

The pressure of my responsibilities leads to irresponsible reactions. An unholy irony. Momma, you don't need to solve every problem, organize every event, or have all the answers *today*. You don't even need to think too much about tomorrow! There is a season for everything. God holds time in His hands, and He will lead you and your family through the next hour, the next day, week, month, and year. Look at your agenda as a beautiful display of God's guidance and provision. Every color-coded entry is a God-created opportunity for blessings.

Lord, I hate it when I get short-tempered simply because I'm looking too far ahead and stewing over how I'm going to do it all. You never intended for me to carry my burdens or get caught up in what's next. I want to be fully present today and look at the fullness of my calendar as a blessing. Help me be more hopeful about what's next instead of stressed. I want to be joyful and kind toward my kids, even when chaos begins to creep into my soul. Calm me. Refresh me. Reassure me that You go before me and that all will be well. In Jesus' name, amen.

## PUT IT INTO PRACTICE

When your kids come to you in a moment when you are feeling stress about your responsibilities, think of it as a signal to stop, breathe, and welcome the interruption to slow down and give your current task to God in prayer. Too often we think it all depends on us instead of depending on God. Thank your child for coming to you and tell them how much you appreciate them and want to meet their needs. Rely on God to meet yours while you take time to meet theirs.

# when your child is *different*

*And yet, O LORD, you are our Father.*
*We are the clay, and you are the potter.*
*We all are formed by your hand.*
ISAIAH 64:8

"Spot the difference between these two pictures." Have you ever played this game? Two images are placed next to each other with seemingly identical appearances,but on closer inspection, there are slight variations that require careful examination to detect. Subtle, but evident, something is missing from one image, or there's a different pattern, or the image contains an extra object or detail. In a world where we don't want to stand out from the crowd, being different is rarely embraced.

Go to any park on a sunny day and you'll see children running and playing with wild abandon. They all have similarities, but each one is unique. Comparing them only serves to highlight the variety—and wishing they were all the same would be futile and kind of silly. Who would wish they were all the same? And yet, we often use comparison to measure our worth as moms, don't we? We long to fit in, to know we are doing a good job and, as a result, other people become our grounds for judgment instead of an inspiration or a celebration of what we have and who we and our kids are.

God knows what He is doing. He never ever makes a mistake. We are the moms for these specific children because that is what is best for them and for us. Throughout our lives, we will all undergo transformation. Maturity is the happy result of growing up physically and spiritually. It's a process. Sometimes a slow one. But the best part of the journey is celebrating and valuing how far we have already come and the joy of who God designed us and our kids to be.

Let's not try to re-mold what the Father is shaping in us and in our children. *Go with it.* Let God have His perfect way in perfecting us. Perhaps today, we can release the need to "fix" our kids and instead yield to the gentle but purposeful shaping of their hearts and personalities that God has designed. And when others cast wary eyes our way? Pay no attention. Find your assurance in our creative God who loves you and your child in the here and now.

Lord, I trust You to take the time You need to work in me and in the life of my child. I know You shaped us as we are for a good purpose. Help me find appreciation and delight in walking the path You set before us. I don't want to get distracted by others' opinions. Thank You for making us all unique and giving me confidence in parenting the way You are instructing me. Where I need growth, I ask You to mold my heart. In Jesus' name, amen.

## PUT IT INTO PRACTICE

Buy yourself a small bouquet of flowers or pick several from your own garden. Place them in a vase where you will see them often. Every time you glance at them, let it be a reminder to appreciate the uniqueness of your family. Tell each child what you appreciate about them today and highlight qualities about them that make them special.

# the *blessings* of obedience

*You will experience all these blessings if you obey the LORD your God.*
DEUTERONOMY 28:2

Blessings follow obedience, Momma! See Luke 11:28.

This mantra is one my children can recite with confidence whenever I ask them what happens when they do the right thing. I've seen this truth played out over and over again in my own life. However, there is a tendency in parenting circles to emphasize the consequences of wrongdoing—but raising kids who do what is right only to avoid punishment sets them up to view a parent as their adversary rather than their advocate. I want my children to obey me out of gratitude and love, which is a mirror of the connection they can have with God.

It's a very different relationship when a child obeys to avoid pain rather than obeying because they love and respect their parents. One angle focuses on avoidance, the other on abundance. Behaviorally, one child exhibits an eagerness to please while the other displays a skittish obedience rooted in fear of punishment. Yes, consequences have their place. Discipline and correction are part of every parent's responsibility, but dwelling on the blessings of obedience is a much happier and peaceful way of relating to our kids.

God tells us that when we obey, it demonstrates our love for Him (John 14:15). He assures us that obedience is not burdensome (1 John 5:3). Obedience leads to physical provision of basic needs, like food (Isaiah

1:19). We will have a defender who fights for us against our enemies (Exodus 23:22). Doing what is right opens us up to the love of God and His presence in our lives (John 14:23). Obedience takes us down the path of righteousness (Romans 6:16). God tells us that when we obey, it will go well with us (Jeremiah 7:23). The Spirit leads us on a path of stability when we follow God's commands (Psalm 143:10). We will even have a long and fruitful life when we have a heart of obedience (Ephesians 6:1–3).

When my child is wavering between right and wrong, and I begin to feel triggered, I too need to remember that obeying God by responding with patience and grace is a benefit *to me*—not only to them. Reminding them of the fruit that stems from the seeds of good behavior keeps me in check. I can easily justify my angry reactions, but when I pause long enough to consider the blessings of remaining calm and kind in my corrections, we both benefit.

The mind is a powerful thing, and it's human to focus on the negative. Let's place the rewards of righteousness at the forefront of our minds. Where we focus, we follow. God does not want us looking over our shoulders, paranoid about what punishment will come next. This way of thinking keeps us from grace and mercy. Instead of viewing God as abounding in love, as a Father who views our sins as far as the east is from the west, we expect that if we take one misstep we are doomed. It is God's lovingkindness that draws us to repentance (Romans 2:4).

As we parent from a place of abundance and blessing in our parent-child relationships, joy abounds. Trust grows between us as we show ourselves to be reasonable, stable, and always seeking to do what is best for our child, even if that means discipline or correction when necessary. As we care for our sons and daughters in this way, our words become less careless. The burden of trying to manipulate our kids' behavior fades as we relax into our role as guides, pointing them to obedience's blessings.

Dear God, thank You for being quick to give blessings of obedience. I want to experience Your benefits in my parenting, and I want my child to value them too. Give my son/daughter a desire to do what is right from a place of love and understanding of Your goodness, not because they are afraid of punishment. Father, you have been long-suffering with me and I praise You for Your grace! Make me a vessel to be used by You to bless my child. In Jesus' name, amen.

## PUT IT INTO PRACTICE

Is your parenting style consequence-centered? Create a reward chart or, better yet, an "I caught you doing something good" jar or bucket. Every time you see your child—whether eight or eighteen—living out behavior that is good and praiseworthy, drop a marble or stone in the jar. When it's full, tell them there will be a reward/blessing they will receive for all the ways they obeyed you and God by living out godly qualities.

# becoming a
# *results-free* mom

*And I am certain that God, who began the good work within you, will
continue his work until it is finally finished on the day when Christ
Jesus returns.*

PHILIPPIANS 1:6

When the apostle Paul wrote to the church at Philippi, he spoke with
confidence that not only did God start the good work in them, but He
would continue it. In fact, the good work we do as moms will last long
beyond our lifetime and it will not be complete until "Christ Jesus returns."
That's a supernaturally strong return on your investment, Momma.

If we won't see the completion of our good work until Jesus returns,
we have the freedom to become results-free moms *today.*

Not long ago, I crumpled into my armchair as my kids walked out the
door with my husband for a daddy-adventure day. "Lord," I cried. "I'm not
sure I'm the right mom for my kids." It had been a difficult season. While
I felt like I was growing in patience and even beginning to see that God
was giving me wisdom in my parenting, my kids were displaying signs of
entitlement. It simplified things to sum up my identity by what I could
see in that moment—*maybe I simply wasn't a good mom.* It takes wisdom
to serve our children and simultaneously teach them to duplicate by paying it forward. In the middle of my muddled emotions and insecurities,
I asked God to give me wisdom. The Holy Spirit nudged me to provide

more opportunities for them to exit their comfort zone and begin to get comfortable with discomfort.

Soon a mission trip opportunity opened up for one son to work with underserved children. Another was asked to assist a sickly neighbor by walking their dog and mowing their lawn over several weeks. I put in place a schedule for another child to take over several tasks around the house that had previously been "bonus" chores but were suitable for him to integrate as part of his regular routine. Over time, they began to count the cost of sacrifice. They recognized that their requests to drive them to the pool to see friends or make extra snacks after dinner when they were too tired to do it for themselves were gifts and not guarantees.

Have you ever questioned your role as a mother? You are in good company, Sister.

Give it time. Do the good parenting. Release the results. Trust God to use you to do the next right thing until the time is right for *Him* to finish the work. God will show you, in due time, that He is using you—the perfect mom for the job.

> Lord, I feel like I'm missing the mark in my parenting. While I see progress, I don't see the results I want. My kids still trigger me, and I am not sure I am doing my best for them. Please give me peace and assurance that it's not really my job to change them. You entrusted them to me, and You instruct me to point them to the truth. I know You are working in my heart and in my child's heart. Thank You for the unbreakable promise that You will complete the good work You have started. In Jesus' name, amen.

## PUT IT INTO PRACTICE

This week, find a recipe for making your own bread. As the yeast works throughout the bread, allowing it to slowly rise, let it be a reminder to you that in the same way, parenting takes a childhood to guide our kids toward maturity and readiness. We "knead" their hearts, give them the ingredients they require from God's Word, and allow the Holy Spirit to work it out all throughout the duration of their lives. Enjoy the fruits of your labor with a slice of warm bread and be comforted to know that in the end, God will fulfill the work He started in your home.

# this is what love *does*

*Don't just pretend to love others. Really love them. Hate what is wrong. Hold tightly to what is good. Love each other with genuine affection and take delight in honoring each other.*
Romans 12:9–10

It was a quiet morning and while the other children were off to school, one of my older sons was still home with me as I sipped my coffee at the breakfast table. I had risen long before the sunrise and my brain felt alert and peaceful.

As my sweet teenager sat beside me, I brought up a concern I had about one of his friendships. It seemed like good timing, until he kindly replied, "Mom, I'm going to be thinking about this issue all day in class now. I really wish you would have brought this up later tonight when I can process it better." It never crossed my mind that this idyllic morning was bad timing for a meaningful conversation, but my son's teenage brain is far more alert and receptive at nighttime. Moms are always looking for teachable moments, *but this one was for me.* Instead of being annoyed that he didn't take my words to heart, the Lord was gently teaching me to be discerning.

If we constantly feel perturbed, our children will not believe they are prized, no matter how much we tell them we love them.

I realized that loving my son and honoring him meant being mindful about the different ways our brains function. As a grown woman, I'm most alert in the morning, but my young son is foggy and extra sensitive when he wakes up. Late at night, he's more stable, ready to share heart to heart and listen with an open mind. Showing him love meant overlooking my weariness come evening, readying myself to talk through his day and anything I felt we needed to talk about.

My hope is that my boy always senses my delight. Even at 10:00 p.m. after a long day! This is what love does. It seeks to communicate when the other person is ready to receive. (And may require an evening cup of coffee to do so!) Just the other night, my other teen pounded on the door of our bedroom and urgently told us he needed to talk. I was already in my pajamas, ready to drop into bed. "I need to understand what the Bible says about speaking in tongues!" he pleaded. "And if there are groups of people in other parts of the world that don't know about Jesus yet, how am I going to reach them?" My husband, Guy, shrugged. I stared at him wide-eyed. I honestly thought he was messing with me. He wasn't. I shook my head to clear my own fog and settled in to give him enough theology to satisfy him until morning. I can't make this stuff up, but I'm convinced that my willingness to show genuine love and interest in my children—at any hour—is a part of why we have the sincere relationships we now enjoy.

Perhaps there is something your own child needs you to sacrifice from a place of love. Maybe the Holy Spirit is tugging at your heart with an idea about how you can show honor to them and their unique needs. Parenting is a long series of sacrifices, but they can be done with bitterness and martyrdom if we don't allow God to work on our attitudes. When we do, I'm certain our kids will know our love is sincere.

Heavenly Father, there is no love more sincere than Your love. Thank You for loving me perfectly. Make my heart both loving and discerning toward my child so that I can honor and delight in him/her. Help me to be a good student of my child so that I can show him/her how much I love him/her. Allow my child to see how much I delight in being their mom. I know they are commanded to honor me as their mother, but I show honor to You, Jesus, when I show them real love. In Jesus' name, amen.

## PUT IT INTO PRACTICE

Is there something your child loves to do that you are not quite a fan of? Maybe a video game they play or an activity outdoors? Take the time to ask them questions about it and participate with them this week. Show them how much you delight in them and the things they care about.

# not a *burden*!

*Loving God means keeping his commandments, and his commandments are not burdensome.*

1 JOHN 5:3

One of my biggest triggers is when my kids resist me. Over a period of several months, one son began to adopt a spirit of resistance. No matter how big or small my requests were, he had a reason he could not or did not want to comply. He made a big deal over little things like clearing his plate from the table or moving to the back seat so his brother could get in the car. It was relentless. My husband and I addressed his disobedient behavior in our typical way, but it wasn't having an impact. Eventually, I had to come away for an afternoon with my son and talk to him, heart to heart.

It's a trigger for most of us when kids view our requests as burdensome. We provide and protect, and their protest feels presumptuous. In part, it's due to the natural developmental stages of childhood. Children begin to discover that they have their own mind, will, and desires. This is a good thing! Gently, but firmly, it's our job to point them to the truth that even when they don't want to obey, they are called to do so, and that it's a sign of their love for us and God.

Meanwhile, feeling victimized won't do us any good. When our child disobeys, it's not against us at the root, but against God. This should not surprise us. All of childhood will be one season of discipling our kids after another. In all honesty, we must examine ourselves to make sure that our own obedience to God in raising them in the Lord does not feel burdensome to us either, lest we find that we are not much different than our kids.

During my son's oppositional stage, we went out for frozen yogurt and while we sat in the shade of a striped umbrella, enjoying the summer day, I lovingly opened a conversation outlining that obeying us was in his best interest, and that more importantly, it revealed his love for the Lord, and for us. I reminded him that Mom and Dad's boundaries are part of God's protection and provision for him. The conversation did not end there. Day by day, I became more intentional to draw his attention to all the goodness that accompanied righteous choices.

On a regular basis, I witness the blessings of obedience. I've learned to actively look for them and praise God for His goodness. It's a spiritual discipline I want my children to embrace and understand at their core. This goes for us too as parents when we patiently and lovingly point our kids to the truth about God's commands and our authority as parents. We don't wield it as a burden, but instead hold our kids accountable so that they can experience the wonderful gifts of doing what is right.

Lord, I want to be quick to obey You, and to think of Your commands as blessings rather than burdens. I know that this must start with me in my heart first, before I can instruct my child. Please help me model the joy of obeying you, God! Soften my child's heart so that they begin to see and take delight in obeying me. Let them experience the blessings of obedience, so that they can live life to the full. In Jesus' name I pray, amen.

## PUT IT INTO PRACTICE

Take a few minutes to reflect on a time when you obeyed God, especially if it was not easy. What was one of the blessings that came from your obedience? Take a few minutes today to share that example with your child.

# rest in *busy* seasons

*Then he lay down and slept under the broom tree. But as he was*
*sleeping, an angel touched him and told him, "Get up and eat!" He*
*looked around and there beside his head was some bread baked on*
*hot stones and a jar of water! So he ate and drank and lay down*
*again. Then the angel of the LORD came again and touched him and*
*said, "Get up and eat some more, or the journey ahead will be too*
*much for you." So he got up and ate and drank, and the food gave him*
*enough strength to travel forty days and forty nights to Mount Sinai,*
*the mountain of God.*
1 KINGS 19:5–8.

Summer days were just around the corner and our kids were restless.
They had worked hard all year in school and needed a break. We all did.
All four of our sons had spent the last five months playing multiple sports,
attending church youth groups, and volunteering for organizations in our
community; in short, running here and there with little down time. Even
though we were careful to carve out rest, we felt ragged. Two of our boys
were showing interest in girls, some of their friend groups were shifting,
and they were busy applying for summer jobs. Our youngest son was suddenly crying at random times, recalling memories with his grandma who
lives across the country, or the good old days when his brother used to
study on the same campus.

So many responsibilities. So much fun. *So much emotion.* This Momma
had to continually take my thoughts captive and remember that much of

their complaining and frustration was a normal part of maturing and facing the world. I was in their lives, placed purposefully by God, to soothe, guide, and gently point them to truth about their circumstances through God's Word. *I was also there to feed them well and put them to bed!*

In 1 Kings 19, God shows us that human nature hasn't changed much. When Elijah faced a long season of speaking out against evil and being a voice for God to an unrighteous king, he showed a lot of courage. But then he began to weaken and become weary and afraid. Fleeing a threatening situation and the violent Jezebel, he found himself completely drained, falling into a deep sleep. God, in His compassion, sent an angel to meet his personal needs. He provided "bread baked on hot stones and a jar of water" and even gave him hope for his next steps forward. Moms don't always need to deal a heavy hand to douse drama. Sometimes, as with Elijah, we can provide gentle biblical refreshment in the same practical ways. With warm banana bread and glasses of milk, I got busy creating room for rest and provision of my boys' basic needs. When my littlest began to feel all the emotions bubble up, I wrapped him in a blanket for a cuddle and a short nap.

Not every triggered moment requires a lecture or an action of correction. Sometimes, we need to simply fill a tummy or cradle a sweet head. In this way, we truly are the hands and feet of Jesus, caring for our kids in ways that show that simple loving actions are often the most healing.

Lord, thank You for seeing us in our humanness and providing for our needs. You give us food and water and shelter. Jesus, we feel fatigue in this world. Too often, we are simply exhausted physically and emotionally. Help me to recognize the signs that my kids need to rest or nourish their bodies. I often overthink or overcomplicate some of these situations that are a normal part of life. Allow me to be more in tune with our limitations and provide boundaries of rest for our family. Thank You for caring about every part of our lives. In Jesus' name, amen.

## PUT IT INTO PRACTICE

What's a favorite family meal you all enjoy? Put it on the menu this week and remind your kids that God cares about even the small needs we have—like providing food for us to enjoy and the gift of sleep!

# you are not *alone,* momma

*The name of the LORD is a strong fortress;*
*the godly run to him and are safe.*
PROVERBS 18:10

I picked up the phone and called a woman at my church who taught a class for moms with infants. I knew she would give me the timely answers I was looking for. Her number was on speed dial, and I hit the tab. It went to voicemail. My anxiety began to rise. I was overwhelmed. Frustrated. It was one of those parenting moments where I had no idea what to do with my son and I felt an urgent need for answers. I called another mom from the class who had a son the same age as mine. Voicemail. Again. Five different calls to five different moms later, I felt more at a loss than I knew was possible.

I was already triggered and feeling helpless. Over and over again, by the time the phone would ring four times, I wasn't just triggered, I was angry. *Why wasn't God helping me out here?*

I turned to woman after woman until gradually, I got the message. Jesus became the only one I could call on with a guarantee that He would answer. Proverbs comforts us with the truth that the Lord is a strong tower and that "the godly run to him and are safe," especially when nobody answers the phone. God was inviting me, through unanswered phone calls, to do a holy pivot toward His peace-filled fortress of protection. I wasn't going to get a specific, logical, immediate answer about how to handle my child from a seasoned mentor. I was going to get the reassurance that no matter what, even when solutions are not apparent, I am being taken care of when I feel like I am on my own.

There is a supernatural blessing in the simple prayer, "Lord, I don't know what to do, but my eyes are on You" (see 2 Chronicles 20:12).

What I needed was to recognize that the Lord was always available to me and that when I call on His name, He never asks me to leave a message. As an omniscient God, He has all the answers to my smallest and biggest parenting problems. When I wanted to know how to meet my child's needs, I first needed to meet God in prayer. He would work out the rest, including giving me wisdom at just the right time (James 1:5) or arranging for a helper to be available. He will do the same for you. Momma, if what you are seeking eludes you, perhaps it's time to replace your triggered mind with trust in the Lord that He has you—and your child—safe and sound.

> Lord, I don't always want to wait on You. I want things to be resolved and questions answered. Forgive me for being impatient. Help me use the unsolved mysteries of parenting to turn to You and rest in Your protection. Thank You for reminding me of the power of Your name and for being available when I run to You. Help me have a calm mind so that I will know that You will work everything out. In Jesus' name, amen.

## PUT IT INTO PRACTICE

Does feeling helpless in a specific situation with your child trigger you? I find that when I give away what I think I need, peace comes. For example, if you wish someone would call you and offer a word of wisdom, think of a friend in your life you could call and encourage today. Let her know you were thinking of her and offer to pray for her needs. We may not always know what to do about our situation, but serving others moves us out of discouragement.

# the *right* timing

*The heart of the godly thinks carefully before speaking;*
*the mouth of the wicked overflows with evil words.*
PROVERBS 15:28

Twice this week, I received panicked text messages from my teenagers. One forgot his practice gear for soccer and the other drove off to his baseball game without his uniform, which was still crumpled in a dirty pile in his bedroom, unwashed from the day before. In both cases, I was in the middle of my own work and had deadlines to meet. There is a possible scenario where they would simply have had to go without. Still, I scrambled to locate missing items, run a load of laundry, and head across town to deliver what my kids needed. Mistakes happen. But in each of these cases, this was not the first time, and they knew to expect consequences.

Even though my sons knew their mistakes disrupted my plans, my flesh tempted me to give them a piece of my mind and complain about their irresponsible actions. Experience has taught me that when emotions are high and stress is at a peak for mom or child, that is not the time to teach them a lesson. My first response is grace, followed by love, even love accompanied at the right time by appropriate consequences. I've learned not to parent in the problem, but to wait until nerves are calm and emotions are stable. Parenting in the problem usually leads to more problems. Delaying discipline is not leniency—it's simply wise discernment—and usually leads to receptive, teachable hearts. That's what I'm after!

89

If our pattern needs to change, it will take time. Be patient with yourself. My personality is the sort that wants to deal with things right away. I like quick results, but when it comes to exchanging angry reactions with gentle biblical responses, it's a process. I've asked the Lord many times to hold back my words and keep me from saying *the right thing at the wrong time.* Learn to circle back, Momma. The wisdom and correction that you have to share will be far wiser and more correct outside of the immediate conflict.

> Lord, Your timing is perfect. Help me become masterful at saying the right thing in the right season that I may mimic my Master. I don't want to be impatient because of my need to get my thoughts off my chest. Make me more sensitive toward my children. Thank You, Lord, for giving me discernment so I can trust Your timing, not mine. Please soften my child's heart as they see me bearing with them and being long-suffering. Never let them take advantage of my grace, but grow to honor me even more as a result. In Jesus' name I pray, amen.

## PUT IT INTO PRACTICE

The next time your child is experiencing stress and heightened emotions in the middle of misbehavior or irresponsibility, meet their needs. Consider their age and then circle back. If they are quite young, it may only be an hour later that you revisit the issue. For older kids it may even be a day or two. In the heat of the moment say this, "I know this is a stressful and emotional moment right now. I'm going to give you what you need because I love you. And because I love you, I will talk with you about this situation later when we can focus and learn to do what is right next time."

# God *hears* and He *answers*

*I prayed to the LORD, and he answered me.*
*He freed me from all my fears.*
*Those who look to him for help will be radiant with joy;*
*no shadow of shame will darken their faces.*

PSALM 34:4–5

The blue skies of Colorado offered an invitation to go for a long walk, and so my friend and I, eager to stretch our legs after a long day of sitting in meetings, headed out to a nearby coffee shop. About five minutes in, we realized our error. Yes, the mountains against the bright skies seemed warm and radiant, but the temperatures were deceptively low, and the wind whipped through our thin layers of clothing until our skin stung with pain. We all but ran to the front door of the coffeehouse and stood inside, momentarily stunned as we tried to recover from the cold. These California girls didn't know that the sun could shine so brightly yet withhold its warmth.

Bright doesn't always mean what we think it does. Not in this world. I feel like this in my home sometimes. The morning starts off with happy sounds—coffee brewing, toddlers cooing, and giggles echoing faintly down the hallway. But all it takes is one mean word, one request ignored, or even a simple missing sock for the seemingly rosy moment to wilt. It took time to discover, but as I searched the Bible, the key to joy in any circumstance was evident. I learned that turning to Him was the way to become "radiant with joy," even when the attitudes of my kids were like dark clouds swirling around our home.

It became a practice, not an occasional whim, to look "to Him for help." My natural reaction when my kids are crying over their hairstyle or stirring up drama with their siblings is not to stop and pray. My flesh reacts easily, and I start my eye roll or stomp my feet in frustration. I've been known to say something dismissive about their emotional outbursts. Every time I give in, the "shadow of shame" darkens my face. No doubt about it. Matching my child's unreasonable outbursts with my own is an unreasonable reaction for a Spirit-filled mom. Guilt follows angry reactions; that is, unless we have become so hardened that we feel nothing at all. God doesn't hide solutions from us. Prioritize time with Him and give Him your fears, needs, and frustrations and yes, your triggers!

God will turn to you and free you from the storm clouds of parenting. When I looked to the sun that day in the Rocky Mountains, I did not receive the warmth that I needed. But with the Lord, we always come away radiant when we turn our faces, and our triggered hearts, to Him.

> Lord, I know that even when I fail and give in to my triggers, You still offer me Your forgiveness and grace. I do not want to keep walking into the darkness of my guilt. Help me take my thoughts under control so that I can learn to look to You in any situation and receive your radiant joy. I cast off the cloak of shame I have been feeling, and I know You will work in my heart today to become calm and kind, even when I am triggered toward anger. In Jesus' name, amen.

## PUT IT INTO PRACTICE

Do you have a hard time stopping in the middle of your triggered emotions to pause and ask God to help you have a gentle response? Practice outside of conflict. Today, each time you make a meal, stop doing what you are doing and thank God for His help in keeping you calm and kind. As we continue to practice this godly habit, it will be automatic when times are not as peaceful.

# remembering the *good*

*"Then I recall all you have done, O LORD;*
*I remember your wonderful deeds of long ago."*
PSALM 77:11

My best friend, Joanne, and I have matching necklaces that hang around our necks: delicate vintage roses in sterling silver that symbolize a saying we have cherished going on nearly thirty years now. "Remember God's roses, Amber!" Joanne will say when I'm at a loss for what to do with my teenager. "Count your blessings!" she will remind me when my world feels like it's falling apart. When I can't understand my husband's actions or control my child's behavior, she asks, "What can you focus on right now that God is asking you to do?" For Joanne and me, roses are remembrances of all the good when things feel bad.

What feels bad today, Momma? I've learned over the many years of parenting that so much of what our kids do is beyond our ability to fix or mold quickly. Good parenting often yields a harvest many years later. We don't always see it right now. The future looks shadowy and unclear. But the past? The present? It holds many answered prayers, many gifts we never even thought to pray for! Stopping to "smell the roses" isn't just taking delight in the everyday moments around us; it's also an opportunity to recollect the ways we have seen God do wonderful things for us before to strengthen our hope and faith for the future.

Just yesterday, my husband tucked a dozen delicate roses into some greenery in the vase on our kitchen table. As I write, I observe the furled edges of each exquisite petal and delight in the creative beauty of God. Outside, the clouds are gray, and rain will soon fall, but the roses remain protected, stretching toward me with all their beauty. Regardless of what will happen outside as the weather worsens, the roses preserve their delightfulness. It would be easy for me to keep looking out the window to predict the first drops of rain or wind, but instead, I can choose to fix my eyes on what is lovely, pure, and nurtures peace in my soul. My roses!

In the middle of your triggers, be intentional to remember *your* "roses." Unlike the flowers we place in vases, the blessings we already have in the form of our children and the incredible generosity of the Lord to meet our every need will never wilt or fade away.

> Lord, I remember all the ways You have met my needs in the past. Even today, I can be thankful for _____ and _____. I know that You have already been helping me in my parenting and guiding my path. I get consumed by my frustrations too often and I forget that You have blessed me and my children repeatedly. I know You will continue to be our Helper. Thank You for loving me even when I forget to acknowledge my blessings. I want to be the kind of mom who is quick to focus on the positive, even when my kids are being immature or unkind. Help me cover offenses with love and remember happier times so that my perspective is balanced. In Jesus' name, amen.

## PUT IT INTO PRACTICE

Spend five minutes going down memory lane with your child. Remind them of some of their blessings. Share some of yours with them. Pray together and thank God for His active presence in your lives!

# when nobody is *happy*

*Obviously, I'm not trying to win the approval of people, but of God. If pleasing people were my goal, I would not be Christ's servant.*
GALATIANS 1:10

Your job is not to please everyone, Momma. There is a longing in my heart to shield my kids from difficulties and disappointments—to do my best to give them their hearts' desires, even though I know that trials are often for their good. But God reminds me my peace comes from pleasing *Him*. Not by pleasing my children.

The other day, I felt like a hostage negotiator, but the captive wasn't a bank employee. It was me. I felt like I was being held against my will to the demands of everyone around me. My intentions were good. My kids' needs were mostly valid. Still, no matter what I did, it wasn't enough. I couldn't be *here* and *there* at the same time. The dinner I prepared made only three out of five happy, the undershirts I had bought were not soft enough, and nobody could agree on a family movie.

One by one, these obstacles seem like normal family dynamics, but on days when it piles on at once, I come away feeling like I'm losing at parenting. It's in these times that I turn to the truth that I'm not supposed to please mankind—or my little men. My heart is to do well by them. To not only meet basic needs, but to give good gifts, as good mommas do. But even then, the desire to please God must override our efforts to please anyone else.

When I start to feel like I can please no one, I can begin to feel like I'm a disappointment to the Lord too. It's my vulnerability that cracks open the door to the enemy's accusations. He likes to tell me I'm good for nothing and that I don't have what it takes to be a great mom. He's evil and a liar. His words are the words of an enemy, disguised as my own misgivings.

Let's fight back with what we know is true. God is well-pleased with us. He is our strength and ultimately the provider for our kids' needs too. God never asks us to always save the day because then our kids might not need a Savior. Our shortcomings, however well-intentioned we are, become opportunities for our kids to look beyond what we can provide in our limited way to the unlimited care and provision of their heavenly Father. Rest in that and do the best you can. It's more than enough.

> Lord, I am not required to be everything for my child. I don't want to remove the need for their dependence on You because of my unwillingness to let them experience a bit of discomfort now and then. I trust You to keep my identity in You and not in how my kids or others view me. You are the only one I need to please. Thank You for loving us in all our shortcomings and for giving me peace when I feel like I'm not the mom I want to be. In Jesus' name, amen.

## PUT IT INTO PRACTICE

Is there a task that your child could easily do if you showed them the steps and let them practice it under your supervision? What's one area where you keep meeting a need that could legitimately fall to your child? Take the first step to teach them how to do it themselves.

# the Lord's *comforting* light

*You light a lamp for me.*
*The LORD, my God, lights up my darkness.*
PSALM 18:28

Every morning, once the sun is up, I tour our home like an inspector, looking for any lights or fans left on in my kids' bedrooms and their bathroom, flipping off the switches to save energy and money. We all have our battles we pick, and while I want my kids to be responsible and turn "all the things" off when they leave a room, I admit I haven't gone hardcore on this one. So nightlights glow in daylight unless Momma turns them off.

We mommas keep the home fires burning, even if we work outside the home. I didn't know that I'd become weary to the bone from both the physical and emotional responsibilities of motherhood. *It's a lot, isn't it?* We feel anything but bright and cheery sometimes. The world looks like it's having the time of its life on social media and here we are, watching other women frolic on beaches while we fester down in the dumps.

If you are anything like most moms I know, we all experience seasons when we feel like we are doing all the nurturing and pouring out, with little return. We long for moments of rest or for someone to take our hand and make decisions so we don't have to.

The darkness has to go when light comes near. Momma, when you feel like the darkness isn't just dimming the room where you turned off the light, but that it has actually crept stealthily into your soul, take heart that the Lord lights a lamp for you. God lights up your darkness! While you manage your little ones, He is near, ready to brighten your path, your heart, your home. Imagine Him, taking your hand, tenderly guiding you toward a cozy couch, illuminating the room, and beckoning you to enjoy the light of His Word as you refresh and restore. There is no darkness of the soul that is beyond His light and love.

Lord, You care for me while I care for my children. You are a loving parent to me, and You light up my darkness. Sometimes I feel sullen, and I don't even know why, especially when it feels like one day is bleeding into the next without much variety. Thank You for lighting a lamp for me—for bringing light and love to my heart and soul. Help me remember that in Your presence, the darkness has to go! My burdens are lightened by Your light. In Jesus' name, amen.

## PUT IT INTO PRACTICE

Tiffany-style lamps are known for their beauty, reminiscent of the stained glass designs found in cathedrals. Imagine a stunning lamp like this, or a spectacular chandelier with valuable crystal sparkling and twinkling its lights all around you. When responsibilities begin to darken your mood, pause and reflect on the light that is reflected from these lamps and take a moment to thank the Lord for His willingness to lighten your mood and to provide for you as you provide for your children.

# welcoming the opportunity for *growth*

*If you love me, obey my commandments.*
JOHN 14:15

I'm a rebel and I know it. I can trace my stubborn and resistant heart back to my early days of motherhood. I knew the right things to do and say, and then, in the middle of responding, I revolted and did the opposite. It's not that I wanted to rebel. It was just so easy, so natural, to do so. God gave me my children to refine my rebelliousness into my redemption.

During my days as a teacher, I learned to be patient and calm when my students were unruly. I thought I had it all together, but God could see the parts of my heart that I had not yet surrendered. My sons' tantrums made me justified in my mind to throw an adult version by huffing and puffing and blowing my house down. It grieves me to say I was often impatient, unreasonable, and self-centered. Being a mom tested me, revealing where I needed God's help to mature. Kids have a way of bringing us to the end of ourselves, exposing what's hidden in our hearts. At first, I wanted to "fix" my kids, so *I* didn't have to be different, but it was in transforming me that everything changed.

Nearly eighteen years later, I have grown in ways I don't think I could have if I had not been a mom. The sacrificial love that motherhood requires purifies our hearts if we allow it to. While God delights in giving us good gifts—such as our children—He knows that along with our joy in them comes opportunities to grow us in holiness. I see God continuing to mold my heart after His, shaping me into a woman who does not shrink away when I'm called upon to die to my own comfort when my child needs me to give them consolation in the dark hours of the night, or asking me to be brave as I loosen my control over my teenagers. God knows that my obedience to Him is evidence of my love. The fact that He doesn't let me stay stagnant in my sin is evidence of His.

God is a good parent. As He deals with our weaknesses, He teaches us how to imitate Him. And when it feels overwhelming to face our faults, He reminds us that He loves us in our childishness and is committed to helping us—and our children—grow into maturity. As we obey His commands, we cultivate love for Him that overflows from our souls and revolutionizes our homes.

> God, thank You for showing me what's in my heart, even though it's hard for me to see. I don't want to settle for angry reactions or any other ungodly words or actions in my mothering. Forgive me for rebelling against You. I want to obey Your commands. It's exhausting trying to think I'm right when I know in my heart that I am wrong. Being a mom requires loving sacrifice and yielding to what is right instead of holding on to my anger. I release it now, in this moment, and I will obey You. I love You, heavenly Father. May You see the evidence of my love when I parent with gentleness and kindness. In Jesus' name, amen.

## PUT IT INTO PRACTICE

Is there something in your home or car that needs to be fixed? Have you been putting it off? Take a step toward repairing it this week. As you do, remember that a peaceful home begins in your heart with your willingness to obey God, not in "fixing" your child.

# when your child *rebels*

*I will give you a new heart, and I will put a new spirit in you. I will take out your stony, stubborn heart and give you a tender, responsive heart. And I will put my Spirit in you so that you will follow my decrees and be careful to obey my regulations.*
EZEKIEL 36:26–27

Do your child's unreasonable reactions to your reasonable requests make you, well . . . *unreasonable* in return? When we feel like we are on a merry-go-round dealing with the same old circles of conflict with our kids, it's not so merry. Hopelessly, we tell ourselves we will always struggle with our strong-willed child who relentlessly challenges our good-hearted parenting with their hardheaded obstinance.

I remember straightening my shoulders and bracing myself every time I asked one particular son to help with the dishes or take out the trash. Like clockwork, he'd say, "I'll do it later, Mom." If I insisted he comply right then, he'd simply ask another child to do the job. Although I took time outside of conflict to discuss my expectations and the biblical necessity for his obedience, I was getting nowhere. Even with consequences in place, his natural reaction was to resist. *For weeks.*

It left my heart bruised from his constant pushback. As long as I took it personally, believing that changing my son was solely up to me, I felt triggered. During that season, the Lord spoke to me tenderly as I sat before Him with my Bible in my lap, asking Him for help. He revealed to me that it was His job to use His Spirit to convict and mature my son. It would be God's responsibility, not mine, to soften his stony, stubborn heart into a tender, responsive one. God wanted me to return to my childlike trust in Him.

Be patient with God's process in transforming your child. In our fast-paced world, we have lost our appreciation for slow growth. If the evidence you seek is not immediately obvious, resist the urge to feel despair. God will complete the work He started in both your heart and the heart of your child (Philippians 1:6). Rebellion rarely lasts forever, but the eternal reward of trusting God for results in your parenting will never end.

> Lord, it feels like my stubborn child is making me more stubborn. I want to be the example of calm but firm as I hold him/her to obedience. Please help me recognize that it's not personal and that my own heart is being exercised and strengthened by these challenges in my home. I trust You, Lord, to reign in my heart and to give me the same heart that You have toward my child. In Jesus' name, amen.

## PUT IT INTO PRACTICE

What good will it do to match your child's stony heart with your own hardness of heart? Go back to your childhood. What did you need in those moments when you were being stubborn and immature, and what would have helped you the most to begin yielding? Gather a few stones from your yard or a nearby park. Place them where you will see them often, such as near a sink or on an open shelf. Each time you see them, remind yourself that God can, and does, give us a beautiful promise that He will give us tender and responsive hearts. Then, pray for your child's heart to yield to God's tender molding.

# you *belong*

*You are citizens along with all of God's holy people. You are members of God's family.*

Ephesians 2:19b

When I was growing up, we didn't have much extended family, but many of my friends did, and occasionally I was privy to how their families operated. I longed for the familiar gatherings of grandparents, aunts, uncles, and cousins that I saw them enjoy. They were the lucky ones, roaming about from one affectionate or endearingly goofy relative to another. I marveled at the gifts and traditions they shared, as well as the special vacations they took together.

And more than that, there seemed to be a sense of security within the happy parameters of the Chavez, Parker, or Floyd families. They had someone to turn to when the chips were down, or a crisis hit. *They belonged.*

My husband, Guy, and I felt the void as we started our own family. It was unsettling to me to feel like I didn't have a generational legacy to draw wisdom from, and so I questioned my parenting choices routinely. It even created resentment in my heart until God, in His kindness, allowed me to see that I am a part of *His* family and that although blood relatives are wonderful, I needed to recognize the blessings and benefits of my brothers and sisters in Christ.

Are you feeling a little lonely today? Missing a sister or grandparent and wishing you could ask them how to handle the anxieties and woes of parenting in this season you are in? Or maybe you have a mom or dad who has unexplainably removed themselves from having any more to do with you. When our own flesh and blood reject us, it can throw us into questioning our self-worth. And there's nothing good that comes from feeling unlovable and unlikeable when we assign more value to man's opinion of us than God's. I know that feeling well, but we are not at a loss. Not really. God has placed us strategically in His family tree. The tangled roots of our family of origin do not restrict us from blooming within the garden of goodness in the family of Christ.

Seek out the wisdom and comfort from the family of believers. Commit to a small group at your church or provide your back patio for the youth group's summer cookout. Give away what you long for yourself and you'll never be lacking. Part of our journey away from feeling triggered in our parenting is feeling cared for and secure, to both give and receive within the fellowship of like-minded believers. There is a place we belong. God's family has the DNA of our good Father, and He will place us in the lives of those who will fill in the gaps, both for their good and ours.

Dear Father, I know that You designed the body of Christ as a family and that I am part of Your household. Thank You for loving me and providing family for me that isn't always a part of my family of earthly origin. More than that, I know that we all have a necessary part to play as a blessing to one another. Please provide friends and mentors that feel more like family! In the meantime, Lord, I need to feel Your nearness today. Wrap me in Your loving arms and keep me close. Help me be a good sister to others in the family of Christ. In Jesus' name, amen.

## PUT IT INTO PRACTICE

One of the best ways that I turn around my feelings of frustration when I'm lacking something I need is to offer to others what I wish I had for myself. Is there someone you know who may not have a lot of friends or family living nearby? Is there a neighbor you wave to but have never gotten to know? Take the time today to send them a message, write a note, or give them a call—like a kind parent or sister would do in the family of God.

# momma, you are not *disqualified*

*Honor your father and mother. Then you will live a long, full life in the land the LORD your God is giving you.*

EXODUS 20:12

God, in His wisdom, set us in our families and established order. I've heard the saying "Cleanliness is next to godliness," but I sometimes wonder if "orderliness" is a better fit for the phrase. Moms and dads are positioned authoritatively over our children for good reason. Along with time and experience comes maturity and wisdom. We have the privilege to love and protect our kids, not just from the world, but from themselves. The promise is clear: When kids honor their father and mother, it leads to a full life!

Maybe this is why we become so incensed when they lack common sense and dishonor us. We expect respect and when we don't get it, the injustice begs for correction. The problem is, too many times we let their behavior influence us and we unravel emotionally. That's the wrong order of things, isn't it? It should be our patience, grace, and gentle spirit that influences our child more than their disobedience influences us. Our faces turn red and flushed at the thought that they still can't behave in the way we want them to. This is the moment when we shift from focusing on their sin to making sure we don't display ours. We get to cover our sons' and daughters' disgraceful behavior with our grace. There is no need to overreact. In fact, it's often our lovingkindness that draws them to repentance, just as

God's generous love covers our own angry reactions (Jeremiah 31:3).

You see, our displays of anger cause our child to become angry *at us.* We give them a reason to focus on *our* behavior instead of giving them room to reflect on *theirs.* And that's what we are after—children who know when they do wrong and are quick to turn away from it because of their love for us, not because they fear our wrath or criticism.

It's not natural to look at our child who struggles to obey with compassion, but that is always how Jesus looks at us in our triggered moments. When we stand with condemnation written all over our face, He overshadows our shame with His mercy. I want to remind you that God made you a mom for a reason and that it was not a mistake. Your struggle with anger has not disqualified you from being an honorable mom. We must, however, consider that we want to honor God with our own obedience that we too may live a full life.

> Jesus, I know that You deserve honor. I don't want to dishonor You when my child dishonors me. Help me stop and consider a right response so that I don't multiply the wrongdoing of my child. I want to live my life knowing that there is no limit to the capacity of what You can do in me and in my home. And I want that for my child! I haven't realized how my own angry reactions have robbed my child from teachable moments. I ask for Your forgiveness, and I receive it. I want to overflow with orderly wisdom and grace when I feel dishonored. I know You will help me. I love You, Lord, and I realize it is your lovingkindness toward me that draws me to repentance. In Jesus' name, amen.

## PUT IT INTO PRACTICE

Have you ever explored your family tree? Make a drawing with as much information as you have of generational lines on both sides of your family. If need be, start with you and your child. As you do so, consider how intentional God was to organize your family line and give Him thanks for being a God of honor and loving authority.

# steadfast *spirit*

# Spirit-led *parenting*

*Fathers, do not provoke your children to anger by the way you treat*
*them. Rather, bring them up with the discipline and instruction that*
*comes from the Lord.*

Ephesians 6:4

It's hard to examine ourselves, isn't it? It was humbling for me to realize that some of my child's irritability and disobedience stemmed from a heart that was being provoked by my own sin or errant mistreatment. Broken promises, especially small ones, were easy for me to disregard. But each time I sinned it had a negative impact on my child.

I say this very gently and tenderly: the attitudes and actions that we have allowed to become normalized in our parenting when they should be put to death may be the reason our homes feel dysfunctional. If our child is often angry, it stands to reason that we may very well be provoking them. It's human nature to want to look outside of ourselves to justify our wrong behavior—or even our ignorance and unwillingness to face the reality that we have contributed to the problems our kids are facing—but waves of grace overpower the undercurrent of turmoil in our parent-child relationships. Humbly acknowledging our part in the triggered atmosphere of our homes begins with us but ends with blessings for everyone under our roof.

Momma, is it possible that some of the things you do and say are directly linked to the way your child misbehaves? Are you willing to go before the Lord and ask Him to work in your life consistently in this area before you begin to instruct or coach your child toward their own righteous behavior? As we invite the Holy Spirit to make His home in our hearts, He convicts us about the way we manage our homes.

In Ephesians 6:4 we see a beautiful exchange taking place. I've seen my children's anger fade away when my behavior becomes righteous. Godly parenting leaves room for us to bring up our children in the "discipline and instruction that comes from the Lord." And moreover, it makes room in our child's heart to receive the truth of the Word of God instead of being crowded out by anger toward us. Do not be discouraged by this thought. Thank the Lord for revealing this to you, and humbly allow His lovingkindness to lead you to repentance.

> **Lord, forgive me for wanting to deal with my child's anger before I deal with my own. I do not want to provoke my child to anger because of the way I treat them. I have been oblivious to how my own sin has influenced my child to become angry. Please forgive me and change my heart. Jesus, You are my Friend, and I know that as my Friend, You will come alongside me and help me treat my children in a friendly and kind way. Thank you! I do not want to exasperate them any longer! Lord, as You change me, remove any poisonous anger or resentment toward me in my child's heart, and repair our relationship. In Jesus' name I pray, amen.**

## PUT IT INTO PRACTICE

Has God brought to mind one thing you do or say to your child that you have allowed to continue even though it is wrong? You may have just prayed the prayer above, and you can trust that God will give you the discipline and instruction you need to repent. Today, be intentional to replace the wrong treatment that you have been allowing in your parenting with a gentle biblical approach. Continue in the days ahead to actively put this into practice.

You may need to humbly ask for forgiveness from your child. They may or not be receptive, and that is okay. Give them time to rebuild trust.

# the *rewards* of discipline

*I discipline my body like an athlete, training it to do what it should.*
*Otherwise, I fear that after preaching to others I myself might be*
*disqualified.*

1 CORINTHIANS 9:27

A lack of discipline in our own lives leads to over-discipline in our parenting. Can you relate? The demands become more than we are prepared to meet, so we reach our breaking point and, instead of calm and loving responses, we are quick to react angrily. In the end, the storm swirling around our everyday responsibilities leads to emotional storm damage that may have been avoided.

So much of my parenting felt like attempting to lasso a tornado of activity. When my oldest three sons were ages four and under, the chaos was mostly physical. Those boys did not know how to rest! The moment they woke up, they were on the move. No wonder moms of littles are drained by three in the afternoon! We've been running hard since the "sons" been up. (*Ha, ha!*) As my kids got older, their schedules demanded that I begin color-coding my calendar to keep up with who needed to be where and when. With three ravenous teens in the house, even the endless meal-making felt like a full-time job. Not to mention the financial strain of raising kids that adds to our responsibility load. I had to stop doing what wasn't working and make better plans.

Momma, before we discipline our kids, we may need to become disciplined ourselves. For example: the day feels more manageable when we set our alarms to wake up twenty minutes earlier to start our day with stillness and a good cup of green tea. We may need to organize regular playdates or put together a carpool. Learning from a mentor to budget well with money left over for savings is a wise step in the right direction. I'm a big believer in being intentional with deep breathing exercises to calm my anxious mindset, as well as memorizing soothing Bible verses when tensions are high.

In 1 Corinthians 9:27, Paul reminds us of the value of discipline. It leads to success and victory. Without discipline, we will not be effectively equipped to run our race and win the prize. It's one thing to be disqualified as an athlete, but it's sobering to think that I could miss out on becoming the godly mom I long to be. The good news is, we do not have to succumb to defeat! Motivation is temporary, but the decisions we make to steward our time, money, and parenting practices withstand the test of time—and our tempers. With God as our hope and help, victory is ours for the taking.

Lord, I need discipline in my life. I'm not as organized as I want to be, and I let myself get to a point of frustration because I'm not taking ownership to change what needs to change. I know that as I do my part, You lift me up and strengthen me. Thank You for being a good Father who disciplines me and doesn't allow me to run wild. Help me discipline myself and give me the wisdom I need to pass that on to my children. Forgive me for over-disciplining my kids and let me rest in Your grace. In Jesus' name, amen.

## PUT IT INTO PRACTICE

In what area of your life do you feel most out of control? What are two reasonable solutions to help you become disciplined in this area? Choose one. Tell a friend about your plan as if they are a "trainer" or "coach" so that you have accountability, and then put it into practice.

# is it too *late*?

*Then you will experience God's peace, which exceeds anything we can*
*understand. His peace will guard your hearts and minds as you live*
*in Christ Jesus.*
PHILIPPIANS 4:7

What if I've already done too much damage to my child by my anger? What if he/she will not forgive me? These questions are ones that moms ask with an ache in their heart and sorrow in their eyes. Their shaky voices reveal how shaken they are as they replay their worst parenting moments. The shame we feel when we lose self-control or see the hurt in our child's eyes is heartbreaking.

When we seek God and ask Him to transform us, He always answers. He has not overlooked you in your struggle with being triggered toward anger. The battlefield of our minds is one we must engage in, seeking to remember what is true according to the Bible. Pray and ask God to change your reactions so that they become gentle biblical responses. Then put a better plan in place. Believe that God is able to transform you, and that right now, this very moment can be your turning point. It's never too late to do the next right thing.

Be assured, God guards your child's heart. He protects your child's mind. Growing up, I experienced a lot of emotional confusion. I often received unkind words and as a result walked on eggshells. But I also had parents who took time every week to help me memorize Bible verses. It was that truth that took root in my heart and reminded me who I really am in the eyes of Christ. When words that wound were slung at me like darts, there was a shield in place that contradicted those harmful arrows. God protected my mind and my heart. Trust that God has done the same for your child.

As we rest in that assurance, it's now time to turn and do better. We have the privileged position to speak words of life to our child. God will be our son's or daughter's peace no matter what, but the blessings of being His conduit of love and protection for our child is both His command and our honor. May we join God in guarding the hearts and minds of our children.

Heavenly Father, it's humbling to think that You use me to reflect Your love to my child. Forgive me for my unrighteous anger and words that wound. Let today be the day I turn away from anger and toward peace. Lord, I receive Your peace and I welcome the opportunities for me to be a peacemaker toward my son/daughter. Help me lovingly guard and protect their heart and mind. Thank You that my child is a gift to me. Let me be a gift to them. In Jesus' name I pray, amen.

## PUT IT INTO PRACTICE

There's a familiar story of a parent who took their children out to the back-yard and began placing a nail in a wooden fence every time their child said something unkind to their sibling. Even when forgiveness came and the nails were removed, the holes were still visible. It was a reminder that our words leave an impact and that we need to be careful about what we say. This is a reminder to us as parents as well. Receive God's forgiveness for the words you may have said that have been sinful. God works everything for our good, even when we mess up and say things we regret, so don't dwell on the past. Look beyond the fence into the field of opportunity to protect and build up your child's heart and mind by your example of lovingkindness.

# consistent *praise*

*I will praise the LORD at all times. I will constantly speak his praises.*
*I will boast only in the LORD; let all who are helpless take heart.*
*Come, let us tell of the LORD's greatness; let us exalt his name together.*
PSALM 34:1–3

One of my favorite salad dressings is oil and vinegar. If you've ever combined these two together, you know that if you let it sit long enough, the solution separates and requires a good shaking to blend them. Similarly, two things that don't easily combine are anger and gratitude.

It feels uncomfortable to think about my body language when I'm angry versus when I'm feeling thankful. If I put my hands on my hips and grit my teeth, but then consider something that I'm deeply thankful for, it's hard to keep my posture tense. Like that tasty salad topper, anger and gratitude simply don't blend well, do they?

For many of us, our knee-jerk reaction when triggered is anger. The feelings of frustration overpower us when we don't tap into the power of the Holy Spirit. I have seen God work radically to exchange angry reactions with gentle responses in my own life and in the lives of thousands of other parents through practical approaches to our triggers, but one of the most transformative blessings comes when we stop trying to fix our kids—and fix our hearts on the worthiness of praising the Lord. This is true especially when our kids leave the refrigerator door open again or do a hasty, unsatisfactory job mowing the lawn. The best time to address them is after thanking God *for them*. Gratitude and praise create ideal conditions for loving correction.

Becoming a mom who practices daily gratitude has been one of the quickest paths toward transformation. When I consider this passage from Psalm 34, the psalmist's enthusiasm is unrestrained. When we are effusive with our praise, our triggered hearts are easily diffused. May we, too, "praise the LORD at all times" and in our "helpless" state begin to "tell of the LORD's greatness." Anger and adoration don't mix. For that, I'm thankful.

> Lord, I want to be known for my thankful heart. I even want my kids to be able to say this about me. Please help me recall my blessings every day. Give me self-control to work on the way I think—to be less exasperated and more thankful. God, thank You for showering me with blessings and instructing my heart. Thank You for all the gifts You give that I often forget about. I love You! In Jesus' name, amen.

## PUT IT INTO PRACTICE

It's easy to thank God for the good things that are obvious. Be sure to do that! But today, consider the hard things that in their own way have also been a blessing. Tape a piece of paper to the wall where your family shares meals. Each day for the next week, ask your kids about something they are thankful for and keep a running list. Be sure to include your own responses and center them around your children or role as a mom.

# our *encouraging* words

*Don't use foul or abusive language. Let everything you say be good
and helpful, so that your words will be an encouragement to those
who hear them.*
Ephesians 4:29

God is full of compassion and understanding. He knows our weaknesses, and yet, we are instructed to let "everything" we say "be good and
helpful." What if tomorrow we woke up and, before we tucked our toes
into slippers and headed to the coffee pot, we took a moment to meditate
on this verse and ask the Lord to help us live it out?

When our kids wake up and grunt instead of greeting us, can we smile
anyway? If we burn our fingers making French toast, would we curse and
complain? When our teenagers spout words that hurt our feelings, would
we condemn, or would we get curious? "It sounds like you have a lot on
your mind, honey. I'm here for you if you want to talk about it," we might say.

A couple of weeks ago, as we sat in church before the service began,
I was talking through a friendship issue and giving my middle schooler
some insights on how to handle a difficult peer. After the service, a hand
pressed my shoulder from the row behind us. A woman apologized for
eavesdropping, but she wanted me to know how blessed she was by the
kind way I had helped my fussy boy work through his angst. We may not
always know that what we are saying or doing is noticed, but if we seek
to live out Ephesians 4:29 as a foundational guide for how we interact
with our kids, we may get glimpses of the positive impact of our words to

encourage "those who hear them" beyond our intended audience.

Over a sustained period, our example of "good and helpful" language to our children shapes their hearts in ways our anger never could. It is far more effective than yelling and blaming when we shift to compassion, using love as our primary motivator. Is what you are about to say truly helpful? If not, reconsider and reconstruct. There is great reward in doing so.

Lord, I can feel peace, even now, as I imagine becoming a mom whose words are never foul or abusive. I want everything I say—always—to encourage and to be helpful. Father, You wouldn't ask us to live this out if it were impossible. Thank You for grace when I fall short. I commit to taking this verse to heart and I trust You to help me use my words to reflect Your goodness and wisdom. In Jesus' name, amen.

## PUT IT INTO PRACTICE

Is there a particular child who needs your loving encouragement? Write a short note to them offering them a word of hope or telling them what is special about them. Even if they don't receive it as you wish, commit to believing the truth that planting seeds of life-giving words will be used by God to shape and encourage your child. Perhaps this will become a weekly commitment on your part to reshape your own perspective and transform you.

# responding with *love*

*From his abundance we have all received one gracious blessing after another.*

JOHN 1:16

My son flat out defied me. I had asked him to cut the lawn before leaving to go meet up with his friends later and he simply said, "No. I'm going to take a nap." And just like that, he sauntered up the stairs to his room and shut the door. A bit stunned, my mouth fell open. Then closed. Then it opened. Then closed. No words formed or came out. Just a small sound of surprise.

My boys have learned that blessings follow obedience, and they usually obey. But when they don't, their disobedience is usually covert. Wishy-washy. *Sly.* They try to cover it up. And I'm sure I was the same when I was a kid. But this new, outright, totally confident, utterly defiant and willful disobedience was next level.

I had the option to freak out. I had the opportunity to march right up those stairs, two at a time, and let him know that he was being willfully sinful and that he was going to do what I say or regret it. And he may very well have reluctantly flung back his blanket, given me a piece of his mind, and then proceeded to do a terrible job of cutting the grass. But the Holy Spirit stopped me. I let him go. He slept. I prayed.

Eventually, he came downstairs and sat beside me. "I'm sorry, Mom. I was just so tired. I apologize. Can I mow the lawn now? Is there something else I can do to make up for it?" Calmly, with empathy, I forgave him and told him that I understand that, like all of us, he was going to mess up sometimes. I also let him know that it was hurtful, but that I was fine, and I would cover this offense with love. He knows by now that I often offer mercy along with some new guidelines for behavior or things he can do to make restitution. Case by case, I have learned to let the Holy Spirit give me discernment about when to lean in and expose and address my child's sin and when to pull the covers up.

I've become more comfortable with offering "one gracious blessing after another" from a heart of abundance, just like God has done for me, His daughter. I don't condone disobedience. I allow it to be a signal that my kids need more of my instruction and training in righteousness. They need my grace. Each trigger cloaked in sin is my chance to model grace in the moment and catalog an area of need for the future as I help my kids toward Christlike maturity.

Think of it this way: One trigger at a time. One opportunity to see the need my child has for my loving admonitions. One privilege after another to demonstrate the generous and lavish grace of God toward my child.

Dear God, I forget how much I have sinned against You. Lord, help me be humble in my role as a mom and remember that my kids are not sinning against me. They sin against You. That should grieve me on their behalf to know they are caught up in sin and struggling. It's not about me! Father, help me be abundant in my grace both with my actions and my tongue. Help me help my child see the blessings of obedience. In Jesus' name, amen.

## PUT IT INTO PRACTICE

The next time your child disobeys, hold your tongue for a bit. Take a deep breath. Think about the most recent time you disobeyed God. In an age-appropriate way, tell your child that even though they are doing what is wrong by disobeying, you know that you disobey God sometimes too. Share with your child that God gives us grace when we sin, and tell them that you want to show them God's grace in this moment. No strings attached. Give them a hug—if it's appropriate and they are willing.

# dwelling on *truth*

*[The devil] has always hated the truth, because there is no truth in him. When he lies, it is consistent with his character; for he is a liar and the father of lies.*

JOHN 8:44B

Satan is a liar, and he always twists the truth. One way he does this is through our memories and our thought life. He loves to bring up the past and parade before us all our failures. He will never bring to our recollection anything that glorifies God or offers hope. His mission is to bewilder and discourage us as mothers.

Do you ever go to extremes with your self-talk? I do. One discouraging thought leads to the next until sweeping generalizations wipe away my confidence. "You'll never be a good mom." Or "You always say the wrong thing." Worse, the devil causes us to question God by saying things like, "Maybe He made a mistake." Or, when we petulantly consider if God actually cares about the difficulties in our family. If your thoughts sound more like an enemy than a friend, you can bet who is planting them in your mind.

The devil does not want us to recall the goodness of God or the many ways the Lord has been our help and guide. He does not want us fixated on the blessings and victories we have secured through Christ. He highlights our most hellish moments and tempts us to believe a lie about who we are and how motherhood will always be. The devil is the author of worst-case scenarios.

Momma, do you remember the many times you spoke soothingly

when your child was afraid? How often you drove your kids to playdates at the park? How patient you were when they melted down at the grocery store? How many times have you prayed with great faith over your child when you were unsure what else to do? Do you remember the countless times you fed and bathed and provided for your daughter? Pointed your son to the Bible? Took your child to church? Corrected them with wisdom? The way they slipped their small hand into yours? How it was you they looked for in the stands at their games? The many times your child showed you how much they love you?

Fixing our eyes on Jesus fixes us. It filters our thoughts through truth and robs the enemy of his influence over our thought life. If you struggle to find joy in your mothering, take a walk down the halls of your mind and unlock the doors that lead to peace. In the corridors of your mind are mirrors reflecting the light of Christ, reminders of His faithfulness in the past, and the promise of His eternal faithfulness in the future. Gather the memories of the goodness of God, and as you do, the lies of your enemy become a distant memory.

> Lord, I have a real enemy that seeks to destroy me. He uses my mind and my memories. Please help me be quick to sense his lies and help me focus on what is true—to remember all the ways I have already shown my love and gentleness toward my child. God, thank You for being good in every way and for reminding me of all the ways You have helped me be a loving, godly mom. I trust You to keep the truth ever before me as I raise my child. In Jesus' name, amen.

## PUT IT INTO PRACTICE

Gather two or three items or make a collage of pictures that represent positive memories of times you were a great mom. Spend time thanking God for these sweet reminders of His goodness and how He is at work in your life and in your mothering.

# fight the *good* fight

*Fight the good fight for the true faith. Hold tightly to the eternal life to which God has called you, which you have declared so well before many witnesses.*

1 TIMOTHY 6:12

It's okay to fight, Momma. Fight the *good* fight. When we know that we are in a battle, we are not caught off guard by the temptation to lose our composure. In the spiritual realm, there are battles being fought on our behalf we may not even be aware of, but sometimes, the conflicts become so intense that there is no mistake that we are under attack. Satan can weaken our home by weakening us, and that is when he gains ground. So, fight!

Fighting *with our kids* is a distraction and a misdirection. We do not fight against *flesh and blood*. There came a point in my mothering where I began to recognize that my anger and frustration was meant for my enemy, not my child. The next time your child sins or does something immature but normal for their age, recognize it as an arrow meant to attack your resolve to be a gentle, godly mom. Then raise your shield. Plant your feet firmly on the Rock of Jesus. Adjust your helmet and lift your sword. Then kneel in prayer for your son or daughter, inviting Jesus to help them with their struggles. Attack in the spiritual realm instead of advancing against your son or daughter. They are not the real enemy.

It's one thing to be on the defense, but moms have the great privilege of acting on the offense. Move toward the protection of your children and seek to launch your own arrows. We do so not by shooting bullets from our tongues in anger, but by striking back against Satan when we offer grace and lovingkindness to our children. We win battles by being patient. We take victory by taking joy in the opportunity to love our kids when their behavior is unlovely. We advance when we acknowledge sin with love and empathy. In our child's worst moments, we breathe life into them by telling them we know they will learn and grow from this struggle instead of spewing condemnation over them. Each time you circle them in prayer and speak truth over your circumstances, you take a victory lap, Momma. It's a battle the Lord has already won.

> Jesus, You won the ultimate battle on the cross when You paid the price for our sins through Your death. I often forget that I am fighting a spiritual battle and that I do not need to fight with my child. Allow Your Holy Spirit to remind me that a triggered moment is an opportunity to fight against flesh and blood. Help me be at peace, knowing that even when I fight the good fight, You are my strength and shield. I rest in Your victory. Thank You for fighting for me and with me. In Jesus' name, amen.

## PUT IT INTO PRACTICE

The next time an argument begins with your child, stop right there in the moment and pray. Pray aloud. Quiet your spirit and tell your son or daughter that this is not a battle between the two of you, but a battle you can win in the spiritual realm. It's okay if they are young and do not grasp this; it's more about our response of faith. Kids pick up on more than we realize, and God will use you to show them how to lean on Jesus in every difficult situation and time of need.

# growing *together*

*We are confident of all this because of our great trust in God through Christ. It is not that we think we are qualified to do anything on our own. Our qualification comes from God.*

2 CORINTHIANS 3:4–5

New seasons require new lessons and growth. I often felt like as soon as I had one area of parenting figured out, we were suddenly playing a new game with new rules. You too? Has your daughter suddenly stopped communicating with you and turned a bit moody? Is your normally compliant son acting out and starting to push your boundaries? Are your kids in a stage where they don't get along, no matter what you do? Embracing the constant ebb and flow of the maturing process in our kids is an opportunity for our own maturity to flow steadily forward. When our kids change, we can remain unflappable, undaunted, *untriggered*.

"But I don't feel like I know what I'm doing or how to handle these changing seasons!" you may say. We don't become the moms we are meant to be by remaining stagnant or because our kids are automatically wise and well-behaved. We grow into wisdom day by day, relying on the Lord Jesus to lead us and be our constant guide. It's our "great trust in God through Christ" that stops us in our tracks when we begin to worry that we don't have what it takes to be a good mom.

Quinn recently graduated from middle school. When he was young, he was strong and untamable, a bit like that proverbial bull in a China shop. I didn't want to have a tantrum over his temperament. Everything about him was high-energy, including his love, so I had to be watchful when he was around his much younger brother to ensure he didn't squeeze too tightly or "help" me out by trying to pick him up and carry him around unsupervised. Now that he is a high schooler, I marvel at how God equipped me to be patient with him so I didn't crush his enthusiastic spirit at a young age. When I felt so helpless, God gave me the Holy Spirit as my helper.

And now, God is using that indomitable spirit of Quinn's personality to be a likable leader in his school's Bible club for athletes and to draw students he invites to our church youth group. God matured Quinn over time and used me, his momma, to help nurture and steer all that imma- ture aggression toward something that would be used for good. Back then, though, I felt totally unqualified to handle his big personality. I didn't need to know the future results, I simply needed to trust that God had a purpose in making me his mom. The God who helped me is the same God who qualifies you to be the mom you need to be.

Our capacity to be calm in chaos is not connected to our own efforts, but instead to the limitless capacity of the Holy Spirit to work through us. Instead of seeing our kids' immaturity and our inabilities as reasons to be- come discouraged or question ourselves, let's begin to accept our triggers as opportunities for us to grow and learn, together. God knows what He is do- ing, and He wants to use you and me to help our kids grow into the adults He designed them to be. So, take a deep breath. Give your insecurities a good talking-to and let them know that your security and trust are in God.

Lord, everything You do is full of purpose, including making me a mom. Thank You for guiding me day by day. I don't know what to do about some of the parenting situations I'm in today, but You do. You entrusted my child to me, and I praise You for the privilege and honor of being a mother. I'm qualified because You saw fit to give me this gift, and I will no longer question it. Help me be confident in my role and willing to learn along the way. I trust You to awaken my understanding of this season my child is going through and how to help them mature. I want to be mature in my faith too, and I thank You for making me a mom. In Jesus' name, amen.

## PUT IT INTO PRACTICE

What two qualities of a mother do you value most, personally? You probably don't give yourself enough credit for the good parenting you are already doing with your child. Write down one example of something you have recently done that exemplifies each of the two qualities you just named. Go ahead, give yourself a pat on the back and thank the Lord for the good work He is doing in your life!

# set a *new* course

*Let your eyes look straight ahead; fix your gaze directly before you.*
*Give careful thought to the paths for your feet and be steadfast in all*
*your ways.*
PROVERBS 4:25–26 NIV

Captains know that if their course is off by even one degree, their ship will miss its destination by hundreds of miles. If a correction is not made, it could lead to disaster. Instead of a tropical island getaway, they may find themselves in the middle of nowhere without a speck of land in sight. Maybe like me, you'd like your home to run shipshape, but instead, you feel miles away from the pleasant, peace-filled ideal you imagined.

When I pictured my future children, I promised myself I wouldn't raise my voice or show my frustration when they messed up. No matter how much we want to do the right thing, sometimes, our flesh takes over. Promises are forgotten. Then, regret settles into the fiber of our being, and we may even try to overcompensate for our angry behavior by overindulging our kids. The result is confusion for our children and a roller coaster ride of emotions for everyone. While the highs and lows of an amusement park are thrilling, the ride we take our kids on with our inconsistency is no walk in the park.

How do we get off the crazy train? We set a new course and recognize that where we are headed is where we will end up.

Your path is not fixed. Momma, where do you want to be today? I always wanted my home to be a sanctuary, the home where everybody wants to return to when they are grown. A place to rest your head and your weary heart. When I look back on my most triggered moments, I lost sight of the atmosphere I said I wanted to create.

Becoming a gentle mom means making small course corrections. The road that leads to a godly home cannot be paved with good intentions alone. It requires stepping stones—like deep, calming breaths before speaking, being more playful with your daughter, and starting each day speaking life-giving words to your son. Map out a plan to keep the shoes in a basket by the front door if muddy tracks derail you, seek out a more seasoned woman to disciple you, or as my friend Wendy Speake says, "figure out what you mean to say before you say something mean." These are the tiny but significant maneuvers that keep us between the lines of peace and joy.

Keep your eyes fixed on God and He will never steer you in the wrong direction. An ocean of blessing awaits.

Lord, I want to set a course that leads to peace and joy in my home. Jesus, take the wheel! I want my actions today to reflect the journey I am on toward more godly responses. Thank You for promising that You will help me stay on a path of righteousness and help me with each step. I know that I am not helpless or stuck. I have Your Word as a map to help me and guide me. In Jesus' name, amen.

## PUT IT INTO PRACTICE

If you continue on the course you have set, where will it lead? Print out a map to a location that represents calm and beauty. Put it on display and let it be a reminder to you to change directions when anger and frustration begin to derail you.

# count on *God*

*God is not a man, so he does not lie.*
*He is not human, so he does not change his mind.*
*Has he ever spoken and failed to act?*
*Has he ever promised and not carried it through?*
Numbers 23:19

Promises, promises. I wish I could say I've never broken one. I think that the worst promises I've broken were the ones to myself. "I'll never say 'that' to my child!" or "This time, I will be more organized and get the school crafts ready on time." Each resolve crumbles into ruins and then my day follows suit. It's one thing to be mad at my kids, but a whole other mess when I'm mad at myself.

Momma, be nicer to yourself today. Grace gives us room to grow. Only God is perfect, and He truly sympathizes with us when we fail. See that part in Numbers 23:19 that says, "he does not change his mind"? Well, that also applies to how He feels about you. He already decided that He loves you unconditionally, which is good news considering some of the conditions we get ourselves into.

Recently, I spoke on the topic of anger to a crowded room of home-schooling families at a conference, and afterward there was a steady stream of weepy moms who came to my book table. Over the course of many hours, each one stood before me sharing their shame through the steady flow of their teardrops. They love their kids, and when they are triggered and yell or react in anger, they lose a little bit more of the love they have for *themselves.* The confidence they have for their role as moms and their ability to raise them right melts with each meltdown when they react in frustration.

But our value and our abilities do not depend on us. They are sourced through the matchless power of the Holy Spirit gifted to us by our faithful Lord and Savior. Moreover, we are promised that we are clean and forgiven. Does your self-talk reflect that truth?

How about another promise for you that God will follow through on? Luke 12:31 says, "Seek the Kingdom of God above all else, and he will give you everything you need." So what do you need? Self-control? A practical solution for your biggest trigger? The confidence that your words will bless instead of curse? Read the Word so you can take Him at His word, which is never broken. Seek the kingdom of God by focusing on things of eternal value—teaching your child to memorize a Bible verse with you, resisting the urge to be constantly offended, or serving in the nursery at church when a need arises, for example.

Perhaps one of the reasons we get our knickers in a twist is because of our tangled perspectives: We focus more on the promises we have not kept than the Promise-Keeper who will not fail to transform us into Christlike moms. He does not "fail to act" on our behalf. Your ability to become the mom you long to be is not dependent on the promises you make to yourself, but on the steadfast promises of God.

> Lord, I believe You and I trust You. You will carry through on every promise You make to me. I often feel like I can't change. The guilt I feel crushes my heart. It's becoming clearer to me that this is not how You want me to think. You want me to rely on You to remove my shame and give me a fresh start. Thank You for loving me even when I break promises to myself. Help me today to meditate on Your promises to forgive me, and help me be patient and loving. May I be a mom my kids can count on and be reliable as a reflection of You. In Jesus' name, amen.

## PUT IT INTO PRACTICE

Go ahead. Make a promise to your child today that you will follow through on within the next forty-eight hours. What do you need to set up to make it happen? Who will you share this with, so you have an added layer of accountability? As you follow through on this promise to your child, take to heart that God is fulfilling His promises to you to help you become untriggered.

# God will
# *strengthen* you

*Have I not commanded you? Be strong and courageous. Do not be afraid; do not be discouraged, for the LORD your God will be with you wherever you go.*

JOSHUA 1:9 NIV

For many moms, parenting feels scary and sometimes lonely. It's a new and exciting chapter of our lives but it also exposes our weaknesses. Over the years, I admit I was discouraged, even dismayed at times. Frightened more than I let on. I felt weak from lack of sleep and resources. The unknowns usually troubled me the most. I struggled with my inability to shield my children from hard things, and my fears sabotaged peace as I worried about what may happen next.

There isn't a playbook for every move as moms, but motherhood is the stage where we play out what God commands in Joshua 1:9: "Be strong and courageous. Do not be afraid; do not be discouraged." We don't face our challenges alone. Our Father goes with us "wherever" we go. Momma, motherhood will require you to be strong. It will ask you to be courageous. Joshua reminds us that the Lord is with us as our companion wherever we go, and so whatever we face, we can expect that all will be well, regardless of our feelings.

What is rattling you today? Being unnerved is a setup for overreacting, shouting in anger, and making decisions that have disastrous outcomes.

When our child talks back in a nasty tone, wounding our hearts, God is there. When the lights go out and we lie awake at night, restless with worry about our friendless daughter, God is there. Sitting in a waiting room anticipating test results for our teenager whose health is worrisome, God is there. Where there is fear, God is near! His nearness is all that we need.

We live out God's command in this passage by taking a deep breath and doing the next right thing. Friend, respond graciously when your child is rude. Say, "In our home, we speak kindly even when we are upset. Please try your words to me again, Son." At night, when worry floods our minds, we roll out of bed and onto our knees, asking Jesus to bring a godly friend into our child's life. We take the time to write out all the good things about our child's well-being and reflect on what is true until the doctor gives us more details. And even then, we do not face any trial alone.

Do what you can today, not from a place of making the best of it, but from a place of strength and courage. Embrace the remarkable and constant presence of God, who knows all things and is our help in times of need.

> Lord, I don't want to feel helpless when I know that You are with me wherever I go. Thank You that I am never alone and that I do not have to feel afraid or weak. Please, God, strengthen me so that I don't fall apart! It takes supernatural courage to remain calm when my child is disrespectful. It takes supernatural peace and hope to face the unknowns with my son/daughter. I know You know. Help me to not give up, but to do the next right thing and to trust You for every situation. In Jesus' name, amen.

## PUT IT INTO PRACTICE

Do one brave thing today, even a small thing. Strike up a conversation with a stranger at a store or apply for that volunteer position God has been putting on your heart. As you practice courage, remember that you do not need to be afraid because God is with you!

# persevere with *joy*

*Dear brothers and sisters, when troubles of any kind come your way,*
*consider it an opportunity for great joy. For you know that when your*
*faith is tested, your endurance has a chance to grow. So let it grow,*
*for when your endurance is fully developed, you will be perfect and*
*complete, needing nothing.*

JAMES 1:2–4

My neighbor knocked on my door, a basket of fresh eggs in hand.
It was one of the best perks of living in a small town for two years when
my husband made a brief career move years ago. I loved having generous,
caring neighbors, especially those who were raising chickens! What I
didn't love was how messy my home was and the embarrassment I felt
anytime someone knocked on my door, should they get a glimpse inside.

I often wished for a housekeeper. A regular babysitter. A financial man-
ager. A gardener. *A fairy godmother!* I would have settled for a travel agent
ready to send me off to a tropical getaway. My three young boys looked so
sweet and innocent, but keeping up with them meant not keeping up with
much else. I loved motherhood. I just didn't love my mismanagement of
all the little daily demands of life. I was troubled and it triggered me.

It's not human nature to face troubles and consider them "an opportunity for great joy." But what if we did? What if instead of becoming tense
we became triumphant? We can't ask God to make us better moms and
then balk when the test comes. The test of being triggered is the means
by which our prayers to be gentle moms are answered. That truth should

move us from petulance to praise, knowing it's our triggers that God uses to perfect us.

Do not wish for a trouble-free life. Instead of resisting the challenges in front of us, let's allow them to shape us into the moms we have prayed to become. Your triggered path, and mine, are not to be sidestepped. Lean in, Momma. Persevere with joy. Let's not just claim faith in God. Let's show it by our unflappable stamina and willingness to be refined by our triggers.

> Lord, help me face my triggers head on. I do not face them alone. I know You are at work, right now, in the middle of my troubles as a mother. You are using them for my good, so help me think differently about my challenges. I do want to be a better mom: godly, patient, and known for my joy. Thank You for never giving up on me when times are hard. I love You. In Jesus' name, amen.

## PUT IT INTO PRACTICE

Make a list of the top three troubles you are facing today. Next to each one, write out one way you can practically demonstrate joy or endurance regarding that trouble. For example, laugh when nothing is going your way instead of frowning. Thank God that You can release control and know that He is working everything out for your good.

# constant *compassion*

*Jesus saw the huge crowd as he stepped from the boat, and he had*
*compassion on them because they were like sheep without a shepherd.*
*So he began teaching them many things.*

MARK 6:34

Compassion is a man named Jesus. A godly momma is a woman who represents Him. What if we replaced our irritability with empathy? When Jesus, bone weary from serving the crowds, came upon yet another needy group, He could have bypassed them. Instead, His heart was moved to action. In His eyes, He saw "sheep without a shepherd." Similarly, Momma, you are your child's shepherd, perfectly positioned to teach them about life's hills and valleys with the same compassion that Jesus modeled.

There may never be a day free from triggers. Don't allow that thought to depress you. If our belief is that gentle biblical parenting means nobody needs anything from us, we will always be anxious, discouraged, and prone to anger. Shepherds, however, continually guide and correct with love and sacrifice. Anytime we get to do what Jesus did, it's not a problem. It's a privilege.

In our humanness, we may feel like yielding to exhaustion or taking the easier path around our triggers. We could set our kids up in front of screens or put them off by saying we'll play cards later. Too often we speak harshly in our impatience as we do so. We may busy ourselves with other tasks that are necessary but less important. It's true—our kids will require that we teach "them many things," and the lessons will be constant through the years. They will rely on us to teach them how to tie their shoes, or make themselves an omelet, or open a savings account at the local bank. The moment we set compassion aside, we will behave from a place of resentment and obligation, the ideal setup for being triggered.

Our children need us to show them how to overlook offenses, put healthy boundaries in place with friends who have not been a good influence, and be respectful toward teachers or coaches who seem to favor everyone else but them. It will not come naturally, so we must override our selfish tendencies when teachable moments arise. Yes, protecting time alone for times of peace and nurturing our own needs is healthy, but more often than not, we are called to lovingly pour ourselves out as Jesus did. He did not sidestep the needs of the people He loved. He called them to step into alignment with Him. Compassion is an unassuming trademark of godly leadership. As we lead like Jesus, we embrace our role as shepherdesses of the next generation.

Lord Jesus, I know You understand how tiring it can be to feel like the needs of those around me are constantly requiring more of me. I am not always filled with compassion for my kids like You were toward the crowds who needed You. Please soften my heart. Help me think of these moments as a blessing and not a burden. I want my kids to always feel like I care about them and that I truly enjoy being the one to teach them life's lessons. Thank You for having compassion toward me as You teach me how to shepherd my children. In Jesus' name, amen.

## PUT IT INTO PRACTICE

Think back to your own childhood. Who was instrumental in teaching you some of the most important lessons in your life? Make a list of the kinds of lessons you'd like your kids to reflect back on as the most important lessons you taught them. What is one area you already know they need you to address this week? Take one step toward meeting that need and ask Jesus to give you compassion for them in the process.

# what you *see* is what you *get*

*The grass withers and the flowers fade,*
*but the word of our God stands forever.*
ISAIAH 40:8

God designed moms as nurturers. We pour out in ways only mothers can, and our children are the better for it. But are *we*? Is parenting making us better? We may not even realize it, but if we feel triggered and easily prone to snapping at our kids, we may be allowing parenting to make us more bitter than better.

Whenever we feel like we are living in a state of agitation, we are attempting to parent in our own strength. The drained mom is often an easily triggered mom. Being intentional to refill when we are empty isn't decadent, it's divine. Even Jesus regularly took time to recharge and refresh during periods of solitude to pray during His earthly ministry (Mark 1:35). If you were to see me at the start of the day, years ago when my kids were small, you'd likely see a tranquil mom, serving her kids with a spring in her step and kindness on her tongue, but come evening, you may witness the other side of me: testy and triggered from pouring out as moms typically do. What you see is what you get, but the Dr. Jekyll and Mr. Hyde split personality is in opposition to the spirit of perseverance that God requires of us, whether at 6:00 a.m. or 6:00 p.m.

One of my self-care practices is buying flowers at the local grocery store to group into small, delicate vases and jars placed in rooms around our home. Flowers invite calm, a glimpse of better things when I'm struggling emotionally. Although peonies and daffodils are beautiful, they are only healthy and vibrant for a short window of time. One day their petals stretch forth in all their glory, and the next, they are furled and browned. The signs of death are unmistakable.

Isaiah gives us a picture of the temporal norm of nature and offers a comforting truth. What is it that can help us be consistent in our character? It's the consistency and timelessness of God's Word. When our triggers go unfiltered by God's enduring promises and instructions day by day, anger and disillusionment set in. It feels too hard. And we become hardened too. We may even begin the day with a singsong blessing on our lips, but by midafternoon, we use our tongues to wound—withering our resolve, much like the flowers decaying in our mason jar.

I often say that it takes a childhood to raise a child—that's at least eighteen years! Our season of influence doesn't last forever. These are the days we are given to steward well. When they are young, the days feel endless, and when they are teens, we sense that time is flying past us at warp speed. Just like the rose or the daffodil, our time to enjoy them is limited. Being angry wilts and withers the opportune moments we have with our children. Is your ideal of gentle, biblical mothering fading fast? Do what you need to do to nurture your own personal relationship with the Lord. He understands our weaknesses, but He is able to preserve the beauty of motherhood when we cling steadfastly to the Word of God. From sunrise to sunset, from toddlerhood to the teenage years and beyond, gentle godly responses need not fade or diminish.

Dear Lord, I take pleasure in raising my kids, but I admit that by the end of the day, I'm not finishing well. I'm tired and weary. You want me to take time to rest and spend time with You so that I'm not trying to pour out from an empty vessel. Help me organize my schedule so

I can put in place more of what refreshes me. Thank You for being consistent and stable! I know I can rely on You to help me grow and remind me that this season is a precious gift, not to be missed. In Jesus' name, amen.

## PUT IT INTO PRACTICE

Take the letters from a meaningful word of your choice, maybe even your child's name, and write a sentence that symbolizes how you want God or His Word to be the foundation for your parenting. Here is one example using the word "Bible":

**B**efore
**I**
**B**egin my day,
**L**ord, fill me up with
**E**verything I need to be a godly mom.

# love *is* . . .

*Love is patient and kind. Love is not jealous or boastful or proud or rude. It does not demand its own way. It is not irritable, and it keeps no record of being wronged.*

1 CORINTHIANS 13:4–5

Momma, soak in the lavish love of God today. His love for you is patient and kind. He is never rude in His treatment of you, and He will never pressure you or be demanding in His nature toward you. Every thought about you is pure and good. None of your wrongs are being recorded against you. He is a perfect Father, and He is *yours.*

Yesterday's episode of exasperation? That wrong decision you made? God's love didn't fade in those moments. The time you said something you wish you hadn't? God has forgotten it. The bossy way you told your child to "Sit down and pay attention!"? He dealt kindly with you then—and He's dealing kindly with you now.

We are often impatient with our slow growth. We want to be better moms, and right now! But when we snap, God has not lost His patience with us. When we compare our kids to others and judge moms at the playground or in the bleachers, He loves us. When empathy wells up for our child falling asleep in church and we rest their head on our shoulder instead of jabbing them in the ribs, God loves us. Our heavenly Father always loves us whether we are naughty or nice.

The greatest command that Jesus shared with us is centered around love (Mark 12:30–31). When I examine my heart and ask the Holy Spirit to reveal pride, it doesn't take very long for it to surface. If I bark at my son or daughter when they talk back to me or they linger a little too long when I ask them to get in the car, there it is. I justify my rudeness by examining their own flaws first. Instead of the overwhelming grace and love of God, my sin nature is revealed.

Today, let's reflect on the truth that God, despite our worst mom moments, remains kind and patient. God is not keeping a record against us. He just loves us. The more we embrace God's unconditional love toward us, the more we will tear down the conditions we require of others to show them love.

Let love lead your words and actions, not your triggers. God will use each situation you face today to love you. May we do the same for our kids.

Heavenly Father, thank You for loving me in your kind way. You are not raking me over the coals when I mess up. You offer me Your unconditional love repeatedly. Lord, I want to truly feel that! Help me love my children the same way that You love me. God, help me be patient and kind. Change my heart so that it's not so irritated every day. In Jesus' name, amen.

## PUT IT INTO PRACTICE

It's easy to be polite to strangers. We often give more grace and patience to people we barely know than those we love the most. Consider how you might speak and behave toward your child if you didn't think of them as someone you had authority over, but instead, someone you just met. What would being polite to them look like?

# a garden of *beauty*

*I am the true grapevine, and my Father is the gardener. He cuts off every branch of mine that doesn't produce fruit, and he prunes the branches that do bear fruit so they will produce even more. You have already been pruned and purified by the message I have given you. Remain in me, and I will remain in you. For a branch cannot produce fruit if it is severed from the vine, and you cannot be fruitful unless you remain in me. Yes, I am the vine; you are the branches. Those who remain in me, and I in them, will produce much fruit. For apart from me you can do nothing.*

JOHN 15:1–5

For some of us, anger simmers. For others, it boils. Either way, it scorches, and we know it. While I longed for my triggers to release their suffocating grip on me, I also yearned for enjoyment in my mother-child relationship with my sons. I loved my kids, but I didn't love the mom I was turning out to be. It didn't make sense to me that on the one hand I treasured motherhood, and on the other hand, I felt like the gifts of mothering were being buried by my struggles.

I realized that the old life had to die in order for my new life to bear fruit. Blossoms are never forced from the seeds. They are planted, fed, watered, and exposed to the light. Over time, they unfold into something beautiful. Jesus is "the true grapevine" and God is "the gardener" of our spiritual gardens. Each time your daughter hurts your feelings by saying something mean or your son rejects the thoughtful meal you prepared for him, it's an opportunity for you to be pruned instead of put out. Pruning is not a punishment. It's not a mistake. And neither are you. But it may be that today you need to draw a little closer to Jesus so that He rubs off on you.

Maybe you are impatient with your toddler's antics, but even more impatient with the slow pace of the changes God is making in your heart. If we have been asking for growth, Jesus will never dishonor our requests. While sometimes God does an immediate work in us, more often, He wisely gives us what we need, just for that moment, adding wisdom and insight and removing whatever is keeping us from prosperity. When Jesus removes anything that stunts our spiritual growth, it is a gift, not a robbery. We must stop thinking about our triggers as problems and reasons to lash out at our child. More often than not, they are our moment of truth that reveals whether or not we are willing to stop angry reactions setting us off into the weeds, or abide in Christ in the middle of the conflict, allowing Him to walk with us down the path of righteousness.

Do you realize that God wants you in His garden? He sees your beautiful potential and is doing the work to produce good fruit in your mothering. Take a deep breath and let Him flow from your heart as you read His Word and pray each day. There is no need to strive. Your role is to stay connected. His is to give you a tongue of kindness. You get to pray. He always answers. As you read and memorize Bible verses and talk with the Lord in prayer, He is designing an abundant harvest to help you become the mom you desire to be.

Jesus, I know that staying close to You is the key to my transformation. I want to be like You. I want to get to know You more. Help me memorize Bible verses that instruct my responses to my kids. Bring them to my mind when I am triggered. I trust You to remove what needs to go. I believe that You will give me what I need to change. Thank You for doing the work as I trust in You. In Jesus' name, amen.

## PUT IT INTO PRACTICE

Moms get things done, don't we? We manage so many small and big tasks that we just keep muscling our way through the day. Set aside ten to fifteen minutes daily to read your Bible or listen to an audio version on an app. Be still. Absorb what is being said to you by your Father. Don't overanalyze it. Simply seek to notice what your reading reveals to you about God, Jesus, or the Holy Spirit. This one practice will empower you, for we "can do nothing" apart from God.

# *gospel-centered* moms

*Your love for one another will prove to the world that you are my disciples.*

JOHN 13:35

Helicopter moms, hummingbird moms, crunchy moms, homeschool moms—we are often labeled by the kind of mommas others perceive us to be based on stereotypes and characteristics. Most of them are harmless and sometimes humorous. But what kind of mom do we truly want to be known as? When I was a school-aged girl, I often prayed for my future children. Not once did I think *When I grow up, I want to be known as an angry, yelling mom.* And yet, the reality was I often yielded to my triggers.

I love my kids, and I am certain you love yours too. The central message of the gospel of Jesus is love. In John 13, the apostle tells us that it's this characteristic that will stand out the most to a lost world. The first mission field God gives us when we become mothers is in our homes. Jesus designed us to be models of love toward all people, *including the ones who call us Momma.* A mother's faith is her child's foundation until they are mature enough to build on their own. There is no greater binding agent than gospel-centered love.

The world is watching. They will recognize us as disciples of Jesus when they see our consistent love for strangers, but in a world where the family is increasingly under attack and eroding, we will have a remarkable impact for the gospel even more so when they witness our lovingkindness toward our children. We stand out from the angry crowd when we kneel down to offer grace to our sinful son or daughter. The world will notice when we handle their constant questions or demands with compassion instead of annoyance. And we will be unquestionably earmarked as a disciple of Jesus when we do not resort to pettiness and instead model spiritual maturity when our child is immature.

Gospel love is present when we parent gently and biblically. We preach it to our kids each time we respond gently instead of reacting angrily, and we proclaim it to the world when they witness our gracious attitudes. Day by day, our reputation as a gospel-centered mom builds. It's not too late. God has been loving toward us, hasn't He? Let that truth fill your heart and know that even now, God is working to use you as living proof of His unconditional love.

> Dear God, You know I love my child. I don't want to be known as an angry mom. It saddens me to think that my son/daughter would think of me as anything but loving, and yet, I know I have not been distinguished as loving when I get overwhelmed and triggered. Forgive me! Help me to become a mom who is known by her loving nature and to be a light to the world as a result. In Jesus' name, amen.

## PUT IT INTO PRACTICE

Take a few minutes to ask each child how they know that you love them. What things do you say or do that make them feel loved? Reflect on their answers.

# magnificiently
*mundane*

*Dear friends, you always followed my instructions when I was with you. And now that I am away, it is even more important. Work hard to show the results of your salvation, obeying God with deep reverence and fear.*

PHILIPPIANS 2:12

There is a "working out" of our salvation for every believer. It's an everyday demonstration of the way we think and speak and act in our new nature as Christ followers. The moment we are saved, we launch into a whole new way of living *and* parenting! We also experience the gifts of the Holy Spirit and are empowered with the ability to do what Jesus would do. It's a miraculous supernatural sanctification played out in the everyday moments of life.

Our uncooperative kids give us opportunities to cooperate with the Holy Spirit. We become the cooperative ones allowing the sanctification process to mold us into moms who model what a life with Jesus looks like. Love, joy, peace, patience, kindness, goodness, faithfulness, gentleness, and self-control—it's all there for us to exchange for our angry reactions (Galatians 5:22–23). Patience and kindness are just as much an option to us when we are triggered as anger is. In Philippians, Paul the apostle tells us to "work hard," and hard it will be. But nothing is impossible with God (Luke 1:37)!

I remember slumping behind the heavy wooden door of my house, seeing the messy living room, and yielding to despair. I questioned whether

I had it in me to wipe counters, change diapers, and make meals again and again, much less with joy and peace. The thought of a fussy and unruly toddler shoving his baby brother one more time, or seeing one of my kids blatantly run away from me when I called him was enough to anger me. My son wasn't the only one who wanted to run away! In my weakest moments, I had to trust that Jesus would be my strength and that He would help me change my attitude and embrace these seasons of labor with love. I had to ask myself, *Amber, do you even care about allowing your mothering to make you more holy?* In my spirit, I knew that beautiful things were right in front of me if I allowed God to have His way with me.

There is meaning in the mundane and there is magnificence too. Like anything we do repeatedly, our godly responses are shaped by constant practice. The triggers will come anyway. Our willingness to let God mold our hearts and our outlook is evidence that God is already at work in us and in our homes. In the process, we become a beautiful picture of our Savior to our children. There's nothing mundane about that!

Dear Jesus, I want to be like You. I want to embrace the Holy Spirit's control of my emotions! Please shift my perspective about all the mundane work I do in my home quickly. Help me embrace the refining process as I come up against challenges with my child. Please help me embrace this process of struggle and not try to avoid it. Use my triggers to sanctify me and make me a godly woman. In Jesus' name, amen.

## PUT IT INTO PRACTICE

Watch a YouTube video about making pottery. Notice how the creator uses the elements of clay, water, a wheel, and other tools to shape and refine the messy lump of clay into something beautiful. Reflect on how God is shaping you, using the challenges of motherhood to mold your heart into a beauty far more spectacular than a piece of pottery.

# the *ministry* of motherhood

*You can make many plans, but the LORD 's purpose will prevail.*

PROVERBS 19:21

I'm a planner. I like it when I have an agenda and I can tick the day's activities off my list. As a mother, my plans for today must be pliable enough to include the plans of my heavenly Father. And His plans are always best.

Being flexible with our children's need for rhythms in their day-to-day activities is only the beginning. The ministry of motherhood is a long game, a commitment to nurture sustained growth over time. The flexibility required in motherhood tears down our self-reliance and builds up our trust in God. As we focus on raising our kids, God raises us to a new level of maturity.

Just today, my meeting with a podcaster was almost derailed by an untimely meltdown. I set up play dough and stencils for art so that I could jump on the interview in the next room while my son Quade kept busy. Wouldn't you know it, he had been playing happily all morning—at least until I needed to step away for a few minutes. He's old enough to play independently and it's good for him to do so, but instead, he began to require all kinds of items he couldn't reach. One of his other brothers was making himself breakfast nearby, so I asked him to engage with Quade. It went great for one minute and 22 seconds. Then they began to argue over *a ruler*, for goodness' sake. In desperation, I woke up my older son and asked him to play with his youngest brother for twenty minutes and keep an eye on him. Thankfully, my older boy, groggy as he was, didn't complain about being woken up early. He stepped up to serve.

At that moment, I didn't have time to teach a lesson or even provide loving corrections for my two younger sons. *It would need to wait.* But when time is short and so are tempers and patience, it's easy to drop our shoulders and hang our heads in despair. *Why can't things be easier than this? I don't ask for much. Couldn't my kids simply help out this one time?* Have you ever thought these thoughts? *Me too.* But when our heads hang low, we can't see the ripe harvest of opportunity to minister under our own roofs. I love doing ministry! But I also need vision to see the *ministry of motherhood.*

After the podcast interview, I saw that God's plan for me on this day was to minister through words of encouragement to listeners. But it also included ministry in my mothering by modeling patience and creative solutions for uncooperative kids. I was able to speak to my squabbling sons outside of conflict, reminding them that we need to care more about the needs of others than our own—and to show honor to my older son who selflessly gave up his plans for sleep to make room for my requests. More than a smooth morning, I needed to smooth over the hurt feelings and frustrations of sibling rivalry.

Each time I yell and am gruff and grumbly, I'm missing the opportunity to live out what I say I believe about God and faithful living. Our kids are immature. Expecting them to always cooperate is a surefire way to get angry over and over again until we get over our unrealistic views. We were never meant to be free from triggers, but our triggers set us free to live out the fruit of the Spirit in our homes. Each trigger is a ripe opportunity to help our kids learn to do the same. Viewing the everyday conflicts with our kids as growth opportunities changes us from an aggravated state of mind to a happy anticipation of becoming the godly moms we long to be, untriggered and unified with the Holy Spirit's refinement in our lives.

And that's been God's plan all along.

**Lord, help me see the possibilities in the middle of conflicts with**

my kids. I know I don't need to get riled up when my plans for today don't go well. You have everything under control and are working to make me the mom I want to be. There is a harvest of beautiful fruit ready for me if I embrace it. I want to honor You with my parenting and the way I think about my triggers. Help me think biblically and respond gently. Your plans for today are not a mistake or a setup for my failure. I trust You to help me respond with Christlikeness and to do the good work You promise to complete in me. I look forward to seeing the fruit of faithfulness in my home! In Jesus' name, amen.

## PUT IT INTO PRACTICE

Take time to write down three of your biggest triggers. Now, write down what you could "harvest" spiritually through each of these challenges. How is each trigger an opportunity for you to see God working in your life? Picture what it looks like to live untriggered.

Prayerfully ask God to help you and transform you. He will.

Thank you for taking this journey with me. My prayer is that you are encouraged and equipped to be a gentle momma. May your heart be confident in Christ's ability to transform you and bring you peace in any triggered moment. If you'd like to connect, please follow me on Instagram and Facebook by searching for @TheRealAmberLia. On my website, www.AmberLia.com, I offer free resources and further encouragement. Please send me an email and let me know how God has spoken to your heart these last sixty days and share with me how I can pray for you. My email address is Amber@AmberLia.com. God bless you, sweet Momma!

# acknowledgments

Every book I write feels herculean to pull off. It's through Christ alone it ever happens. Still, there are people in my life who come together to support and love me through it.

To my agent, Janet Grant, I remember that first thrilling conversation years ago when you offered to represent me. I'm as thrilled now as I was then. Thank you for advocating for me and giving me your continual godly wisdom.

Judy Dunagan, thank you for being my editor. You believed in this message and understood the felt need. I knew I could count on you to pray for me and for this timely book—these 60 days of hope and encouragement for struggling mommas. I wish everyone could have as skilled an editor as you!

Pam Pugh, thank you for helping me refine my voice and overcome unsightly obstacles through your brilliant role as my developmental editor. This stage can be nerve-wracking, but you made the process a joy for me. I'm blessed to know you.

To the lovely team at Moody, thank you for lending your varied expertise and words of encouragement as we journeyed together to bring *UnTriggered* to the world. I'm forever grateful.

There are those who trudge along with me through the hills and valleys of the writing process—dear sisters in Christ who pray and brainstorm and cheer me on. Wendy Speake, Joanne Ferril, Jodi Arndt, Jess Kalvaitis,

# Connect
# with Amber

You can connect with Amber through her website, amberlia.com.

Sign up for her newsletter and access free resources like her study guides and wellness assessment.

*AmberLia.com*

Amy Shahbaz, and Macki Smith, you have been balm to my soul, time and time again. I love you!

The Lia men . . . Guy, Ollie, Quinn, Oakley, and Quade—I do everything for God and for you. May this book be a legacy and a letter from my heart to yours. I love you boys with every fiber of my being, and I pray that I live out the truths and the lessons in *UnTriggered* in our own home. Thank you for allowing me to share our stories with the world. I love you acres and oceans and buckets and barrels full! Big hugs and kisses!